What others are saying about *The GodSense Journey: Exploring Sacred Pathways:*

"This is a precious gem. I have been challenged, engaged, and encouraged. For many weeks and days, I was in dialogue with the Holy Spirit as I worked my way through the devotional. In reading I was inspired to put the principles into practice. My relationship with Jesus has been deepened. I especially loved how Bev invited me to participate with the ideas in each section. It was a hands-on project. She got me into the Bible and spending more time in God's presence. I have been so blessed!" – Marcia Haslick

"Each day I look forward to starting my day reading this devotional. Each day, I am invited to meditate and learn through Scripture with Beverly guiding me into sometimes new ideas and sometimes reminding me of old ideas, always focusing on Jesus' love, mercy, and grace. I have been blessed by beginning my day exploring sacred pathways." – Carol Shake

" . . . those who read Bev's work will encounter challenge, engagement, and thoughtful encouragement. She has a unique, non-directive style. She sets a defined spiritual framework and an invitational environment, and then the reader gets to enjoy plugging in where he or she wants to. It is a daily invitation to dialogue with the Word of God. The GodSense Journey: Exploring Sacred Pathways . . . will answer some questions, provide renewal and refreshment, and open you to a more fulfilling relationship with Jesus." – Chaplain (Colonel) Michael T. Lembke, United States Army (retired)

Other books by Beverly Van Kampen:

The GodSense Devotional: 52 Weeks to a Transformed Life
The Bible Study Teacher's Guide
The Bible for Skeptics

The GodSense Journey:
Exploring Sacred Pathways

by Beverly J. Van Kampen

with prayers written by Margery A. Lembke

Copyright ©2017 by Beverly Van Kampen
All rights reserved

No part of this publication may be reproduced, stored in a retrieval system, or transmitted in any form or by any means – electronic, mechanical, photocopying, recording, or otherwise – without the prior written permission of the author. The only except is brief quotations in printed reviews or appropriately cited in other publications. Requests for permission should be made in writing through the author's website at beverlyvankampen.com.

Unless otherwise stated, all Scripture citations are from the *THE HOLY BIBLE, NEW INTERNATIONAL VERSION®*, NIV® Copyright © 1973, 1978, 1984, 2011 by Biblica, Inc.® Used by permission. All rights reserved worldwide.

Scripture quotations taken from the *Amplified Bible*, Copyright 1954, 1958, 1962, 1964, 1965, 1987 by the Lockman Foundation. Used by permission. (www.Lockman.org).

Scripture quotations taken from *The Message*, Copyright 1993, 1994, 1995, 1996, 2000, 2001, 2001. Used by permission of NavPress Publishing Group.

DEDICATION

I dedicate this book to Margery A. Lembke, a dear friend and spiritual mentor.

By watching her live, listening in on her prayers, accepting her counsel, and knowing her heart, I was irresistibly drawn into the world of the Spirit. For Marge, there never seemed to be a barrier between the world we see and the world we do not see. Though she is now face-to-face with Jesus in the eternal world, I am still blessed for having known her in this one.

FOREWORD

In 2004 I headed to Iraq as the Chaplain for the 1st Infantry Division. My wife, and I had committed to do a devotional study together as a way of maintaining contact during the twelve-month separation. Prior to my deployment, my mother, Margery Lembke, sent me a copy of *GodSense**, a year-long devotional study book that her friend, Beverly Van Kampen, had just published. She included the following words in the front of the book:

To Mike and Nancy,

You two have set a marvelous example for the transforming power of Jesus. Blessings as you continue receiving new beginnings in your lives.

In His love,
Margery/Mom.

As I prepare to retire from active military service and return to the civilian pastorate, I am happy that Bev has written a companion volume, *The GodSense Journey: Exploring Sacred Pathways.* In this concise, and at the same time, expansive set of meditations, devotions, reflections and prayers, she presents an opportunity to the reader for spiritual, personal, and relational growth, all in the Name of Jesus.

I know that those who read Bev's work will encounter challenge, engagement, and thoughtful encouragement. She has a unique, non-directive style. She sets a defined spiritual framework and an invitational environment, and then the reader gets to enjoy plugging in where he or she wants to. It is a daily invitation to dialogue with the Word of God.

"(The) kind of prayer we here speak of . . . is a prayer of silence, simplicity, contemplative and meditative unity, a deep personal integration in an attentive, watchful listening of 'the heart'." – Thomas Merton

My mother passed away in 2015. I hear her voice in the prayers she wrote for this book and I know the reader will be edified by the moments of spiritual intimacy offered in each petition.

The reader will find inspiration in reading and appropriating the devotional principles presented in this writing. I enjoy writing music and was inspired from the first *GodSense* devotional book to compose a song based on Bev's guidance to "Turn your worries into prayers". If ever there ever was a title for a song that was it! I have sung that tune many times and always get a good response from those who hear it.

Whether you are seeking inspiration, encouragement or are looking for direction and format in your devotional life you will indeed find that *The GodSense Journey:Exploring Sacred Pathways,* will more than meet your needs, answer some questions, provide renewal and refreshment, and open you up to a more fulfilling relationship with Jesus.

- Chaplain (Colonel) Michael T. Lembke,
  United States Army (retired)
  March 2016

*The GodSense Devotional: 52 Weeks to a Transformed Life, FaithWalk Publishing, 2004

INTRODUCTION

This is a devotional book for serious Christians. It is for those of us who long for a closer walk with God, who desire to do His will, who want to learn more about His ways in our world. It will teach you, challenge you, and invite you to grow.

The goal? Spiritual depth, unencumbered relationship with our Father in Heaven, answered prayers, met needs, and full engagement in serving the One who loves us beyond measure.

It is not a traditional devotional in the sense that it is something you read and think about. Instead, you will be invited to engage with the ideas presented, to go to the Bible for further enlightenment, and to spend time in the presence of God so He can apply the teaching in your life as He desires.

Here's how we do it:

I know you are busy – this book is designed for people like you. We take one topic per week and spend a few minutes on it each day. With a short time commitment per day, you should have a good grasp on the topic and its application to your life by the end of each week.

- Each Monday you will be provided with some teaching on a topic related to your spiritual life.
- On Tuesday, you will be given a verse to focus on in a time of meditation, allowing the Holy Spirit to teach you through the Word of God.
- On Wednesday and Thursday, we offer a little more teaching on the topic of the week, giving you something to think about as you go through your day.
- On Friday, you will engage in a guided Bible study.
- On Saturday, you will be challenged with some personal application questions.
- Sunday is reserved for prayer. All the prayers in this book (with one exception) are written by my spiritual friend and mentor Marge Lembke to whom the book is dedicated. You

will be blessed by her moment-by-moment relationship with the Father as you read her prayers.

Here's what you will need:

A Bible: Any translation will do. I tend to use quotes from *The New International Verson, The Amplified Bible* and *The Message.*

A notebook or journal: Because of the interactive nature of this devotional/study, you will need a place to keep notes from your times of Scripture meditation, Bible study, and personal application. If God is teaching you, you will want to write it down so you can revisit later in the year or even years from now as you review ways in which He has moved in your life.

A willing heart: God is a gentleman and, as such, will not force His way into your life. If you want Him there, though, He will come – guaranteed. So be soft towards Him. Invite Him to speak to you and to teach you. Open wide your heart to accept the love that He is so ready to pour into you.

    As you peruse the Table of Contents, you will see the topics we cover. They relate to our privileged position as beloved members of the family of God; our growth in areas such as love, joy, peace, faithfulness, patience; understanding Jesus' life, purpose, and ministry and why it matters today; and assessing how we fit into God's plan for serving Him and others around us. It will be a year of challenges and, if our hearts are open, of profound growth in relationship to the triune God.
    For other inspirational topics, feel free to go to my blog *Walking Together on Holy Ground.* You can find it at beverlyvankampen.com.
    Welcome to the journey! It is my prayer that the Holy Spirit will be your teacher as you join us in exploring sacred pathways that will lead us into His presence where we will experience His generous blessing every day.

                                           Beverly J. Van Kampen
                                           April 2017

TABLE OF CONTENTS

Part 1: Spiritual Formation

1	You Are God's Treasure
2	It's All About Relationship
3	Tuning in to God's Presence
4	The Eternal View
5	Hearing the Voice of God
6	Guilt-Free Living
7	Changing Our Minds
8	Sacred Pauses

Part 2: God as Father

9	Adopted into God's Family
10	Meeting Us in Our Need
11	Family Forever
12	Knowing God, Knowing Ourselves
13	Unlovable? Not to God!
14	No Fear: Protected!
15	Taught by the Great Teacher
16	Accessing Our Spiritual DNA
17	Asking for Help
18	The Family Resemblance

Part 3: Jesus as Word and Savior

19	When God Became Human
20	God's Word in a Body
21	Life-Changing Word
22	The Power of the Word
23	The Ultimate Sacrifice
24	Touching the Eternal
25	Living in Eternity's Light

Part 4: Transformed Relationships

26 Designed for Relationship
27 The Importance of Honesty
28 Risking Relationship
29 For the Long Haul
30 Through the Struggles
31 Learning to Forgive
32 Living Forgiven
33 The Difference God Makes

Part 5: Fruit of the Spirit

34 Knowing God as Spirit
35 Connecting with the Spirit
36 A Genuine Love
37 A Bubbling Up Joy
38 Invitation to Peace
39 The Progress of Patience
40 Becoming Good
41 The Kindness of Caring
42 Under Control
43 The Joy of Gentleness
44 Sticking with It

Part 6: Spiritual Gifts

45 At Your Service
46 Equipped to Serve
47 Recognizing Our Gifts
48 Serving Creatively
49 Finding Time to Serve
50 Leading or Following
51 Rewards of Serving
52 On Becoming

WEEK ONE

You are God's Treasure

"Grace teaches us that God loves because of who God is, not because of who we are." –Philip Yancey

MONDAY

THOUGHTS FOR TODAY

I have a fine pearl ring. Although there may be bigger, better, more beautiful pearls in the world, there is none that is more beautiful to me. Why? Because this is the one my husband chose for me. He found it in the window of a jewelry store and saw the look in my eyes when he showed it to me. He went back to the jeweler the next day to purchase it, though the price was high. Why? Because he wanted to give me that particular ring as a token of his affection. His love drove the decision to pay the price for the ring.

In Matthew 13, Jesus tells of a merchant who also was looking for fine pearls to buy. We are told that he found exactly what he was looking for. It was a pearl of exquisite beauty, one that, in his mind, was unlike any he had ever seen before. He wanted that particular pearl so badly, that he sold everything he had and bought it. The message in that story tells us about God. He is the merchant and *you* are that pearl. He wanted you so badly that He gave His own Son so you could be His. *You* are God's pearl of great price. His love drove Him to give what was most precious to Him to make you His own.

We are pretty hard on ourselves sometimes. We tend to be self-critical. We know our shortcomings and are aware of how much we fall short even of our own standards. We can't even think about being able to meet the holy standards of the God of heaven. Yet, God has a different view of us than we have of ourselves. He looks at you and me as His dearly beloved ones. He infuses us with value and our lives with meaning. He lifts us up, dusts us off, and says, "My dear child, you are my precious, precious treasure."

If we can grasp that concept and make it part of the way we think and live, we will begin to view ourselves differently. Yes, we will still make mistakes, sometimes bad ones. We will still have attitudes that need cleaning up. We will still get discouraged in our walk with God. But the underlying value that God has given us will hold us up. We can know that we are loved, treasured, valued, and worthy, not because we have done anything to earn that status, but because God has declared our value by paying an immeasurable price to make us His.

TUESDAY

MEDITATION

". . . consider the great love of the Lord." (Psalm 107:43b)

Quiet your mind before God and meditate on the words of this verse. Let the great love of the Lord surround you as you ponder these words. Write down any thoughts that come to your mind after a few minutes of quietness before God.

WEDNESDAY

THOUGHTS FOR TODAY

When we think of Jesus' leaving heaven; coming to earth; living among actual 1st Century men, women, and children, and dying on the cross for us, we begin to realize what a great sacrifice He made – for us. He did it all to pay the penalty for the sinfulness of our hearts. He died so we will not be condemned when we face God someday. And, thanks be to God, He was raised from the dead and is preparing a place so we can be with Him eternally.

But there's more to it than that. What was the rest of God's purpose in paying such a tremendous price for us? I think one answer is that He wanted to have this lifetime to work within us and show us what value He places on us, even though we may not be able to see that value ourselves. Our relationship with God does not begin when we die. It begins when we accept the gift that Jesus offers through the payment He made. We then begin to see ourselves as Jesus sees us – valued, treasured, loved.

And this new relationship means that we now can have free access to our Father in heaven. It means that the Holy Spirit lives in us and, if we are willing to listen, will direct our thoughts and actions. It means that we are learning to put off our former way of life and put on the new and better way that is revealed in the Bible. We begin, step-by-step, to become all that God saw possible in us when He identified us as pearls for which He was willing to pay a great price.

THURSDAY
THOUGHTS FOR TODAY

There are two sides to our relationship with God. On His side we find unconditional and eternal love. On our side we are to reverence and obey Him and also to spend time and energy in getting to know Him. Once we realize how much He values us and how much He was willing to do to open a way for us to relate to Him, we are motivated by gratefulness and love to respond to all He has done. Our response is met by a deep love from God and that draws us even closer. It becomes a never-ending journey of God's love, our response, His continued love, our obedience, His gracious love, and our gratefulness.

The Bible is full of passages that tell us all that God will do for those who are willing to relate to Him in this way. Here's a sampling:

"I will never stop doing good to them. . ." (Jeremiah 32:40b)

"I know the plans I have for you . . . plans to prosper you and not to harm you, plans to give you hope and a future." (Jeremiah 29:11)

"And my God will meet all your needs according to his glorious riches in Christ Jesus." (Philippians 4:19)

We are God's dearly loved ones. We are His treasure, His precious pearls. As we live in the light of that knowledge, we grow into the persons He has planned for us to be and we share in His rejoicing over us. No matter what we are going through right now, we have very good reason to be filled with joy. It's a great way to live!

FRIDAY

READING GOD'S MESSAGE

Ephesians 2:1-10

What does this passage acknowledge about our condition before Jesus came into our lives?

How did God feel about us even when we were in this condition? (v. 4)

What does the word *grace* mean to you?

According to verses 8 and 9, what can we do to make ourselves worthy of God's love?

What does this passage tell you about how valuable you are to God?

SATURDAY

FOR PERSONAL REFLECTION

Since you know you are God's precious treasure, think about how you treat yourself:

Are there thoughts you no longer want to allow to stay in your mind?

Are there unhealthy activities or actions you choose to give up in order to better care for yourself?

Are there unhealthy relationships you need to work on or walk from in order to value yourself as God does?

What good things can you do for yourself that would show God that you accept the great value He has placed upon you?

Pray, asking God to help you see yourself as He does. Then ask Him to show you how to live day-by-day in the light of His great love for you. Write down any thoughts that come to your mind. They may be from Him.

SUNDAY

PRAYER

O God of Love, would You give me the grace to receive what is on Your heart? Thank You, thank You for having no ulterior motive or hidden agenda. When I look into Your eyes I see pure love. You are the only one who is able to love me purely. And You are enough! Let this love radiate out from your children to touch the world, this world which You loved so much that You sent us Jesus, Love made flesh. In your mercy, hear our prayer. Amen.

WEEK TWO

It's All About Relationship

"God's love is much more than our human love simply multiplied and expanded. God's love for us will ever be mystery; unfathomable, awesome, entirely beyond human expectation." – Joseph Langford

MONDAY

THOUGHTS FOR TODAY

Think of the happiest moments in your life. For most of us, our happiest memories center on relationships. We think of trips we have taken with our families, days of playing together at the beach, special holiday celebrations, long talks with a spouse, bringing home a new baby, opening our home to guests, and so on. If an overwhelming majority of our happiest memories involve other people, will it surprise you to know that God is like we are that way? He takes great pleasure in relationships. That means He takes great pleasure in relating to each of us!

And because we would not have figured that out on our own, He spells it out very clearly in the Bible which says that even before the world was made, God chose us to be adopted into His family and, then the verse says, "What pleasure he took in planning this!" (Ephesians 1:5 *The Message*). In other words, He put together the plan of salvation and made us His children not because He felt obligated to do so, but because He *wanted* to. It pleases Him to have us close.

As human beings, we like to be with people who like to be with us. If we can see God as someone who loves to have us with Him, we most likely will begin to approach our relationship with Him with new light and new energy.

But, you may protest, "Isn't God to be reverenced and feared? Isn't He the judge of all the earth?" Definite "yeses" to both of those questions. There is nothing like being in the presence of God to reveal to us our own sin and powerlessness. However, we are told that if we confess our sins, we will be made clean and *then* we can experience full fellowship and friendship with God (1 John 1:9). If we take God up on His offer to get the sin question out of the way by honest confession, the judgment of God is no longer something we fear.

We still acknowledge His greatness and approach Him with awe, but as soon as we begin to get overwhelmed with His power, He comes to us as a gentle shepherd or a loving parent and calms our fears. Even though God is holy and mighty, we are invited to come into His presence and sense His smile at our being there even if there's still mud on our shoes.

TUESDAY

MEDITATION

"Mostly what God does is love you. Keep company with him and learn a life of love. Observe how Christ loved us. His love was not cautious but extravagant. He didn't love in order to get something from us but to give everything of himself to us. Love like that." (Ephesians 5:1-2 *The Message*)

Read these verses through several times, then focus on a word or phrase that the Holy Spirit seems to highlight in your mind. Think quietly on those words. Write down any thoughts that come to you.

WEDNESDAY

THOUGHTS FOR TODAY

One of the ways that God shows His pleasure in our company is by making sure that our communication with Him is two-way. We are comfortable in relating to Him in prayer, but if we do all the talking, it's not much of a relationship, is it? In fact, I can imagine God listening as I go on and on in prayer, just wishing I would pause long enough to let Him get a word in edgewise!

God wants to talk! In fact He says, "If you had responded to my rebuke, I would have poured out my heart to you and made my thoughts known to you" (Proverbs 1:23). This is an amazing concept. I have poured out my heart to God many times without realizing that He was willing to pour His heart out to me if I would be responsive to His nudges and would give Him an opportunity to speak.

And then, just think about the benefit to us in being let in on God's thoughts. What greater wisdom and understanding could we have than to know what God is thinking? We simply have to pause to listen. Over time we will learn to recognize the voice of God as He speaks to our hearts and through our minds. The give and take of conversation and the sharing of our innermost thoughts and feelings is what real relationship is all about. And that's the kind of relationship God wants to enjoy with you and me.

THURSDAY
THOUGHTS FOR TODAY

Being there for each other is an aspect of friendship that we value in our human relationships. That same characteristic brings pleasure to both God and us in our relationship with Him. How can we "be there" for God?

Looking at the life instructions He gives in the Bible is one way to gain insight into how we can be His supportive friends. He asks that we live with one another in unity, that we help the poor and needy, and that we spread His message to others in the world. He also asks that we get to know Him and understand His perspective on living our lives and on relating to Him. If we want to please God, we will begin to take seriously the ways in which we can show Him our love. Paul says it this way, "We make it our goal to please him . . ." (II Corinthians 5:9a).

The other side of the coin is that God wants to "be there" for us, too. He tells us to bring our needs and our desires to Him, to talk to Him about what troubles us, and to ask Him to intervene by His provision, His action, His power, and His love. He has promised that, if we do that, He will respond; and being able to give us our desires will bring Him pleasure. ". . . I am the Lord, who exercises kindness, justice, and righteousness on earth, for in these I delight" (Jeremiah 9:24b).

FRIDAY
READING GOD'S MESSAGE
Psalm 23:1-4

Read this familiar passage as if you are reading it for the first time. See in your mind's eye the shepherd and his sheep. Think about these questions:

What kinds of things do you see the shepherd doing to show His care for the sheep?

What feelings are attributed to the sheep throughout this psalm?

How do you think the shepherd feels about His sheep? Why do you think that?

What does this psalm teach your heart about God's care for you?

SATURDAY
FOR PERSONAL REFLECTION

Describe in a few sentences your concept of God.

How does your image of God affect the way you relate to Him?

Do you think that the image you have of God is consistent with what the Bible teaches about Him? How might it need to change?

How do you think adjusting to a more realistic view of who God is might change the way you relate to Him?

SUNDAY
PRAYER

O Lord, our Lord, how majestic is Your name in all the earth! Give me a mind to understand the majesty of Your name. There is power in Your name for all my needs. Let all the complaining and whining leave me, and may I spend my days contemplating the greatness of Your name, the name above all names, that at the name of Jesus every knee shall bow and every tongue confess that Jesus is Lord!

WEEK THREE

Tuning in to God's Presence

"If I find in myself desires nothing in this world can satisfy, the only logical explanation is that I was made for another world."
– C. S. Lewis

MONDAY

THOUGHTS FOR TODAY

The spiritual realm is invisible to us, but it is more real than the reality that we can see or touch or feel. And what makes us as human beings different from other created things is the fact that we exist simultaneously in a physical world and in the spiritual world. If we need insight into any area, it is into the area that is the very real, but invisible, eternal world of the spirit.

One of the reasons we are not more aware of the spiritual world than we are is that we are very attached to the things that we can see, touch, taste, and experience in the physical world. In order to attach to the spiritual word, we must be able to detach from the physical world. Through the years, saints of God have developed certain disciplines which help us to detach in order to attach. They include these practices (among others): contemplative prayer, meditation, study, worship, solitude, simplicity, and fasting. These disciplines are some of the keys which unlock the spiritual world to our understanding. When we place ourselves in the presence of God, Who is spirit, we allow Him to open our awareness to a spiritual realm which we could not access without Him.

If we want to know spiritual truths, we have to open ourselves up to the great Teacher of those truths, the Holy Spirit. We have access to the spiritual world through this Teacher sent by Jesus, but He does not shout above the noise of the world. He whispers, He nudges, He gently guides, and He unfolds truths to us to the extent that we are willing to separate ourselves from the hubbub of our culture, our relationships, our work, and our personal desires in order to listen in the quietness.

Over a period of time, practicing various spiritual disciplines will enable us to do this. Then, this promise becomes a reality in our lives: "Spirit can be known only by spirit – God's Spirit and our spirits in open communion. Spiritually alive, we have access to everything God's Spirit is doing. . ." (1 Corinthians 2:12-13 *The Message*)

TUESDAY

MEDITATION

"The Friend, the Holy Spirit whom the Father will send at my request, will make everything plain to you." (John 14:26a *The Message*)

Meditate on the truths in this statement by Jesus. Contemplate the Holy Spirit as a friend and as a revealer of the truth of the eternal world. Make notes on any insights you receive.

WEDNESDAY

THOUGHTS FOR TODAY

There *is* another world intersecting with ours every day. We usually are oblivious to it, but I am learning that we don't have to be. The Holy Spirit is the door to that world and we often feel closest to it when we pray, or praise, or think on His Word. Another key component for me, though, has been in practicing *awareness*:

- God reveals a little of Himself in the flower we hold, in the waves of the sea, or in the stars on cloudless night. Are we paying attention to His creation?
- God's image is in every person we meet, though they may not know it. Are *we* aware? Are we looking for Him in them?
- There is a bigger purpose behind everything we do and everything that happens to us. Can we sense it?

As we become more and more attuned to the intersecting world, we realize how absolutely real it is. It makes the world we see, as C. S. Lewis also says, seem like "only shadows" of the reality that exists. What is truly amazing is that God sometimes pulls back the curtain to give our souls a glimpse of the invisible.

It is then we realize that our deepest desires can be met *only* in the world we cannot see. A taste leaves us longing for more. Awareness, living mindfully, can help us see the unseen.

THURSDAY

THOUGHTS FOR TODAY

There are places on this planet, where the separation between heaven and earth seems very thin and, in those places, it is said that you can hear God more clearly and feel God more closely than anywhere else. Some see the mountains as thin places, where the peaks reach toward heaven and the majesty of God is revealed. Certain traditions have recognized thin places on this planet where people have met God powerfully through the ages. Retreat centers, churches, and monasteries often are cited.

I believe that we can create our own thin places: For one of my friends, it was her daily hour-long walk where she could talk to God without interruption. For another, it was under the stairs in her home, and another tells me she has her best sense of Jesus' presence on her backyard deck. For me, it is the couch downstairs where I can open the blinds and wait for the dawn as I read His Word and listen for His voice.

Of course, we can meet Him anywhere along life's path (and we do!), but for those of us who have been on the journey for awhile, we find there are sacred spots where God seems to break through with ease. Do you have a place like that? If not, I hope you will create one as an invitation to sacred encounters every day of the year!

FRIDAY

READING GOD'S MESSAGE

Genesis 28:10-17

Under the guise of finding an acceptable wife, Jacob is running away from his family home. In reality he has stolen the birthright and inheritance from his brother, Esau, and Esau has vowed to kill him.

He is camping near Luz for the night when the event described in this passage occurs.

Describe his dream.

What promises concerning offspring and land did God give him in this dream?

What promise did God give Jacob concerning His presence?

What was Jacob's emotional reaction to the dream when he awoke?

Think about this sentence from verse 16, *"Surely the Lord is in this place, and I did not know it."* Jot down any thoughts that come to mind.

SATURDAY
FOR PERSONAL REFLECTION

Have you ever felt God's presence in a particular place? Explain.

If God is everywhere, why do you think we don't notice His presence more often?

What is one thing you might do to help develop a greater awareness of God's constant presence?

Have you ever had a dream that seemed to have a spiritual message? Describe it.

Have you ever thought to invite God to speak to you while you sleep? It might be a good prayer as you fall asleep tonight.

SUNDAY
PRAYER

Holy Spirit, soul of my soul, thank You that You speak in a still, small voice. This forces me to quiet my mind, quit the frenetic pace, slow down and listen. You never yell or are harsh or unloving. No wonder I desire to hear Your voice over anyone else's. You speak words of life, change, transformation and offer me a new way to live. Thank You for letting me get to the end of my rope so that I could turn to You; I can praise You for all the dire circumstances of my life because You showed me how to walk through them with hope, expectation and even glory. How shallow life is without suffering. Without Your suffering, Jesus, we would not have life. Continue to lead on, my glorious suffering servant. You alone have the power. Amen.

WEEK FOUR

The Eternal View

"Life on earth matters not because it's the only life we have, but precisely because it isn't – it's the beginning of a life that will continue without end." - Randy Alcorn

MONDAY
THOUGHTS FOR TODAY

The Pilgrim's Progress is an allegory written by John Bunyan to help us understand the journey we embark on when we become followers of Jesus. The main character is Christian who runs from his home in the City of Destruction and begins his pilgrimage to the Celestial City. He encounters joys along the way, but also many difficulties including the Slough of Despond, the Hill Difficulty, Vanity Fair, Doubting Castle, the Valley of Humiliation, and the River of Death. He meets people he can trust and those he cannot. He learns, he struggles, he fights, he grows, and eventually he comes, with great joy and by God's grace, to the Celestial City where he will live eternally with God, angels, and other saints.

The message that we sense in this story is the troubles we face in this life are simply part of the spiritual pilgrimage we all must make in order to be able to mature in our faith, while we look forward to dwelling forever with Christ in the comfort, love, and security of our eternal home. In Bunyan's mind, and consistent with Scripture, the existence of eternity gives meaning and purpose to all that we endure in our short years here on earth.

There is a world outside of the world we see. It is not imaginary. It is very real and it intersects with our physical world, though we cannot see it. Jesus described it to Nicodemus (John 3) as being like the wind. You can't see it, but there are evidences of its existence if you are paying attention.

TUESDAY
MEDITATION

"**So we fix our eyes not on what is seen, but on what is unseen. For what is seen is temporary, but what is unseen is eternal.**" (2 Corinthians 4:18)

Let the Spirit who lives in you bring light to these words as you meditate on them today. Focus your internal eyes on the eternal. Write down thoughts that come into your mind.

WEDNESDAY

THOUGHTS FOR TODAY

What would our lives be like if there were no spirit world? No Holy Spirit? No angels to guide or guard us? No angels around the throne of God in heaven? Do we ever stop to realize how we acknowledge and rely upon the world we cannot see? Our lives would be pretty shallow if all there was to reality is what we can see with our eyes.

Helen Keller, blind and deaf from just after birth, used to say that the most important things in our lives, the things of lasting value, were the things that we could not see with our eyes. She was right.

Think about your earthly relationships. Those most valued are the ones which we might call "heart-to-heart". What we really mean is "spirit-to-spirit." Our spirits are who we really are, the core being without the restrictions of body and place and time. Our spirits are the part of us that will live forever in the presence of God who is also spirit. As one wise soul once said, "We are spiritual beings on a human path rather than human beings who may be on a spiritual path." (1)

This human path will someday end. Then we will know life as God created it to be - without sin and all of its crippling effects. Most of all, we will be in the presence of God. Our deepest needs will be met, we will be perfect, joy-filled and will gratefully worship Jesus who made it all possible.

THURSDAY

THOUGHTS FOR TODAY

Here are some truths revealed in Scripture about the reality of the unseen world:

- There is a spirit world even though we cannot see it.

- That world consists of both good and evil spirits.

- Through Christ's victory on the cross, the world of evil spirits has been subdued and is given freedom to act in this world only under the authority of God.

- Someday the entirety of the world of the spirit will be revealed and the spirits of evil will be cast from us forever.

- When the real world of the spirit is revealed, those of us who follow God will begin our eternal lives with Him and His angels in Heaven and on a new earth – the true world for which our spirits long.

In the meantime, we have access to the spirit world through the Holy Spirit Who protects us and Who communicates with us through our hearts and our minds. This indwelling Spirit carries our prayers to the throne of God, reveals truth to us, and whispers words of God's great love to our hearts.

Without the spirit world, our lives would be temporary, shallow, and meaningless, and they would end when we die. Because there is a spiritual world and because Jesus has given us the victory, we have no fear of Satan, his demons, and his lies. We trust, instead, in the power of God and the strength of the Holy Spirit and know that our lives have meaning and power and eternality because God's Spirit is greater that the spirit of this world.

FRIDAY
READING GOD'S MESSAGE

2 Corinthians 4:16-5:10

Read this passage and think about these questions. If you have a copy of *The Message* (you can find one free online at Biblegateway.com), you might gain additional insight by reading these verses in that version as well. Think about the contrast the writer, Paul, draws between our temporary life (represented by the tent) and our eternal life (represented by the building).

How does the writer (Paul) separate the world of the flesh and the world of the spirit in 4:16?

How does he contrast this earthly life and our heavenly life in 5:1? Which does he say is better?

What is the purpose God made us, according to 5:4-5?

What is the goal of our life, knowing that we are made for eternity (5:9)?

How does this teaching affect the way you look at what is on your "to do" list today?

SATURDAY
FOR PERSONAL REFLECTION

What is the biggest problem you are facing in your life right now?

How does having an eternal perspective help you to deal with it?

If the world of the spirit is the real world, how would you describe the importance of prayer in dealing with that world?

Spend some time in prayer asking God to reveal the real world to you as you go about your life today. Ask Him to help you see people as eternal beings in need of the Spirit's power. Ask Him to use you to affect the real world and not just the temporary world which we can see

SUNDAY

PRAYER

Jesus, You are the only reality. I cling to You, my Jesus, because only with You am I able to keep an eternal perspective on what is real and what only looks real. How empty my life would be without You. You alone are life. Thank You for dying so I could experience Your life now, in this present reality. Thank You for sending the Holy Spirit, my secret weapon against the world system's onslaughts. We pray with holy fervor that everyone would choose to have this spiritual discernment and receive the Lord Jesus as Savior and Lord. That is Your will. We pray in Your holy name. Amen.

(1) Jean Shinoda Bolen, *Close to the Bone* (SanFrancisco: Red Wheel/Weiser, LLC. 2007), p. 19.

WEEK FIVE

Hearing the Voice of God

"The kind of prayer we here speak of . . . is a prayer of silence, simplicity, contemplative and meditative unity, a deep personal integration in an attentive, watchful listening of the heart." –
Thomas Merton

MONDAY

THOUGHTS FOR TODAY

Does God speak to us today? I believe He does. God is not hiding. He wants us to connect to Him and He knows that words are the way we understand best. We have evidence that God communicates with those who love and follow Him. The Bible is full of examples of people with whom God talked directly: A few examples include Adam, Abraham, Noah, Joseph, Moses, Samuel, David, Mary, and Paul. We know that God never changes, so it is safe to assume He still communicates to you and me. First, let's think about the purposes God may have in speaking to us today. There are three that come immediately to my mind.

To reveal a truth He wants us to know. Jesus told His followers that, after He left this earth, the Holy Spirit would come and would guide them (and us) into all truth. Jesus defined Himself as truth and the Spirit would be sent to reveal truth to us. That revelation of truth comes through the Bible, but it also comes in an understanding of circumstances in our lives, of the true character of God, of our condition before Him, and of our relationship to Him and to others. One way we can understand those truths is by communication from the Spirit of God within us.

To direct our service for Him. God has a plan for this world and it is His desire to use us, as human beings, to carry out that plan. To that end, He is willing to speak to those who are tuned in and obedient to Him so direction can be given for His work. Have you ever been talking to someone about a problem in his life or about spiritual issues, and suddenly you realize that the words you are saying are not a pre-thought-out speech, but just seem to flow from somewhere deep within?

When we are walking closely with God and that happens, I believe that the Spirit is speaking to us and we are sharing God's message with the person to whom we are talking.

To strengthen our relationship with Him. God knows that we need encouragement. When we earnestly seek Him, He said that He would be found. "Call to me and I will answer you and tell you great and unsearchable things you do not know" (Jeremiah 33:3). God wants to share His heart with us and to enable us to know Him better. All He asks is that we call on Him.

TUESDAY

MEDITATION

"Whether you turn to the right or to the left, your ears will hear a voice behind you, saying, 'This is the way, walk in it.'" (Isaiah 30:21)

Think about these words and ask the Spirit to apply them to your heart. What does God reveal about Himself in this verse? Write out your thoughts.

WEDNESDAY

THOUGHTS FOR TODAY

God's messages to us are usually whispers. We have to be very quiet and attentive in order to hear them. How do we prepare to hear the voice of God in our lives?

Make the time to cultivate an intimate personal relationship with Him. Sometimes we hear God as we go through our days, but only if we have learned to recognize the sound of His voice by listening in the quietness of our times alone with Him. We must make sure our prayers are two-way communication. We talk to our Father in heaven, then we listen for His response.

Listen for him continually. As we engage in the activities of our lives, we learn to be attuned to God's voice. He will direct our paths, speak through our thoughts, and bring verses of Scripture to mind.

Worship Him for being who He is. He knows that when we

praise Him, we open pathways of communication so He can reveal to us more about who He is and what He desires in our relationship to Him.

Deny yourself. Want His will alone. God says we will find Him when we seek Him with all our hearts. That means, we listen for God's voice not for our own selfish purposes, but only to know Him, to submit to His will, and to be act on His direction.

THURSDAY
                THOUGHTS FOR TODAY

When God speaks to us, we must take His message very seriously. When we hear His voice through the Bible, we might consider responding this way:

Write down, for word, the passage of Scripture that spoke to us.

Meditate on it when it is first given and throughout the day.

Pray the passage or verse back to God; listening for further insights.

Be obedient to any command the Scripture gives.

Watch for ways God uses that particular verse or passage in our lives that day.

Write down what we sense God is saying to us.

Watch for God to confirm His message through the Bible, through circumstances in our lives, or through another committed Christian.

Obey what we sense He is asking us to do.

Thank Him for revealing Himself to us.

There are times that we can more clearly hear God's direction when we are praying with other Christians. God's will plus unity among believers gives authority and power to our prayers (Matthew 18:19-20). When God speaks to us as part of a united body of believers, we are more able to confirm the message that is given. We are not relying solely on our own understanding, but can depend upon others to confirm what we believe we are hearing. God loves to have His children working together!

God's people who listen to God's voice in God's way will live in power, light, and understanding and, in so doing, will be changed and will become agents of change in our world.

FRIDAY
READING GOD'S MESSAGE

Acts 10:1-32

What two people does God speak to in this passage?

How did each react to the direction God gave?

What method(s) did God use to speak to Cornelius? To Peter?

How did these two men confirm the messages they had received from God?

What does this passage tell you about God's desire to communicate to people?

SATURDAY
FOR PERSONAL REFLECTION

Have you ever sensed God speaking to you? If so, how did you react? Write down your experience.

From what we have learned so far on our *GodSense Journey*, list several ways in which you can cultivate your ability to hear God's voice. What is one thing you are ready to put into practice this week? Is there any area of your life about which you are not willing to hear God's direction? If so, give that area up to Him today so the communication between you and God will have no barriers. You can trust Him.

Write down any insights that you believe God is giving you about steps you need to take to grow a more intimate relationship with Him.

SUNDAY

PRAYER

Holy Spirit, soul of my soul, I'm so thankful that You have a voice. It is a loving and authoritative voice, but it is not an authoritarian voice. It denotes love in the fullest way by letting me choose. There is such freedom with You, Jesus. I heard You speak to me on a subject today where I wasn't getting what I wanted from You; You asked me, "Will you trust Me?" It was up to me to answer "yes" or "no." You also said, "I have a purpose and a plan." It did comfort me to be reminded of that and I saw that You still had my best interest at heart. You were gracious to show me that You are worthy of trust. Forgive me when I doubt; I want to be done with doubt, Lord. I trust You. I pray in Your precious name, amen.

WEEK SIX

Guilt-Free Living

"To be able to look into God's face, and know with the knowledge of faith that there is nothing between the soul and Him, is to experience the fullest peace the soul can know. Whatever else pardon may be, it is above all things admission into full fellowship with God." –
Charles Brent

MONDAY
THOUGHTS FOR TODAY

Knowing God, listening for His voice, and becoming more intimate with Him is our goal. But there is a problem that arises: It is sin and sin is the great separator. It separated Adam and Eve from God in the garden. And, if we do not deal with it, sin still separates us from God and, often, creates conflicts with other humans. Jesus came to bring about a way to bridge the separation that sin has caused. When we accept Jesus' gift of a way back to God, we know that our sins have been forgiven. The God whom we once feared now is the God whom we enjoy and love and talk to. And, once we are restored to relationship with God, relationships to other humans can be healed as well.

It's a great plan, but there seems to be a problem. We keep sinning. And in doing so, we keep separating ourselves from God and others. If we could only be perfect! Or, better yet, if only the people around us could be perfect! But perfection is just not going to happen in this world. While we are here, we will have to deal with sin. God knew that would be the case and He provided a way for us to take care of the sins that we keep on committing in spite of our love relationship with Him. There are several things to keep in mind as we look at the concept of confession and forgiveness.

First, it is God's desire to forgive us. "At the heart of God is the desire to give and to forgive. . . Love, not anger, brought Jesus to the cross" (2). Jesus came so we could be forgiven. We do not need to hesitate for even one minute to come to God in confession of our sins. Forgiving is what God does.

Second, the Holy Spirit will convict us of sin (John 15:8).

What we call conscience is often God's Spirit talking to our hearts and telling us that there is sin in our lives we need to confess. When He talks, we need to listen and respond. God's forgiveness is available, but we can receive it only after we acknowledge and confess our sin.

Third, God has promised not only forgiveness, but also healing and restoration. When we confess our sins, we find that the consequences of our sin may not be taken away, but our hearts can be healed. With all this promised, we are foolish to resist the Spirit's promptings and to continue in our sin. There is no sin that is worth turning away from the wholeness and freedom that God's forgiveness promises.

TUESDAY

MEDITATION

". . . return to your God! You're down but you're not out. Prepare your confession and come back to God. . . I will heal their waywardness. I will love them lavishly." (Hosea 14:1-2;4)

Meditate on these words, pondering the great love of God. Ask the Spirit to convict you of any sin that you may need to confess so that God can heal you and love you lavishly.

Listen, confess, be cleansed, thank Him. Make some notes in your journal.

WEDNESDAY

THOUGHTS FOR TODAY

Suppose we are aware of a particular sin that seems to have us entangled. We don't want to do it anymore, but we are not sure we can overcome it. Yet, we realize that it is wrong and we know that it is affecting the fullness of our relationship with God. It may even be hurting someone else. How do we go about confessing this sin?

First, in a quiet time before God, we must take responsibility for what we have done. No excuses. We allow the Spirit to show us the full extent of our actions and experience true sorrow for what we have done and the pain it has caused us, God, and others.

Then we simply agree with God that what we have done is sinful. We confess our guilt and we ask for His forgiveness. And even if we know we will be tempted, we determine that we will not commit this sin again. We will focus, instead, in our renewed relationship with God.

Now, we get to celebrate. We can enjoy the feeling of cleanness and sense God's pleasure in our commitment to Him. We know that we can live free from the power of this sin over us if we will stay plugged in the power source of the Spirit. We are free, happy, and beginning to experience the wholeness God has promised those who live in close proximity to Him. It doesn't mean that we will not sin again. But we now understand that confession, while painful, leads to joy. Isn't God's plan great?

THURSDAY
THOUGHTS FOR TODAY

There are times when it is good for us to confess our sins not only to God but also to other Christians. Jesus, in fact, gave authority to his followers to offer forgiveness on God's behalf (John 20:23). Why is it helpful for us, sometimes, to confess to another person?

First, talking aloud about the sin helps us to deal with it truthfully. We sometimes need another's help in seeing our sin completely. By speaking it out, true light can be brought to bear on the problem and we can make a fuller, clearer confession.

Second, receiving the forgiveness is sometimes easier when it is offered through another person. There are times when we find it hard to believe that we are forgiven. Having another affirm that forgiveness can help make it more real to our hearts.

Third, there is a healing power that is released when we confess to one another. James 5:16 says, ". . . confess your sins to each other and pray for each other so that you may be healed. The prayer of a righteous man is powerful and effective." Do we understand the order there? First confess to God and to each other.
Then we can be declared righteous and, in that condition, our prayers have power. Healing comes.

Finally, having the strength to overcome the sin we are confessing is easier when we become accountable to another person. We are stronger when we are working together.

FRIDAY
READING GOD'S MESSAGE

1 John 1:5-10

How does John compare light and darkness to truth and lies?

Why is it important to walk in the light of truth if we are to live in close relationship to God?

How are we made pure by walking in the light? (v. 7)

Will we ever become sinless in this life? (v. 8)

What will God do if we come to him in confession of our sin? (v. 9)

SATURDAY
FOR PERSONAL REFLECTION

How can the Spirit help you distinguish between false guilt and genuine guilt? Think about times you have experienced both.

How can you make sure you have a balance between the need to be forgiven and an unhealthy preoccupation with sin?

When is it acceptable to confess your sins to God only? When might you need to confess to a fellow believer?

When someone confesses a sin that they have committed against you, are you able to forgive? Why or why not?

Spend some time in prayer following the steps of confession we talked about earlier this week. Then vow to keep short accounts with God, confessing sins as they occur so you can always have open relationships with God and with others.

SUNDAY
PRAYER

Father, I will take the time, which is a gift from You, to slow down and listen to Your love. Your love draws me to You and makes me want to be like Your son, Jesus. His heart of love woos me and gives me such a strong desire to please You. There is no other love like Your love; You never reproach me for coming to You with sin and all my baggage. All You ask is that I agree with You about my sin and then I can walk in the light with You. I give up my rebellion; it was killing me. Thank you for the message that Your strength and Your power go with me because I'm your child. Thank You, too, for other believers in Christ to walk with me on the journey to transformation. Nothing is too hard for You. You are the God of the impossible. I praise You for this good news. You are Lord! Amen.

(2) Richard Foster, *Celebration of Discipline, 20th Anniversary Edition* (New York: HarperCollins Publishers, 1998), p. 143.

WEEK SEVEN

Changing Our Minds

"There is a simple gazing at the Lord while the heart reaches out in wordless prayer and the will seeks to be one with His." – James Borst

MONDAY

Contemplation does not come naturally to us as human beings. We tend to be busily involved with a whole list of activities that keep us from sitting still before God. But while stillness will require an effort on our part and goes against the natural flow of our lives, it offers benefits that can be accessed in no other way. There are many times in the Bible that we are told to meditate. The concept of thinking, pondering, and listening was one that biblical writers assumed we would understand and make a part of our lives.

Before we talk about the forms of contemplation, let's take a look at how developing this practice can benefit us. First, slowing down and focusing on the things of the Spirit gives us *balance*. There is much about the world we live in that causes anxiety, creates distress, and encourages us to keep going at breakneck speed. Jesus told His disciples to come away from the crowds and rest awhile. He does no less for us. Contemplation, meditation, and thinking on the things that bring peace to our souls cannot be done in a hurry. The quietness of sitting before God offers balance and will bring into order the pace of our lives.

Second, God promises *peace* for those who keep their minds fixed on Him and His Word. ". . . whatever is true, whatever is noble, whatever is right, whatever is pure, whatever is lovely, whatever is admirable – if anything is excellent or praiseworthy – think about such things . . . And the God of peace will be with you" (Philippians 4:8 and 9b). This is mind control at its best: forcing from our brains the negative, unwholesome thoughts, and filling them instead with the thoughts that allow God's peace to rule in our hearts.

Third, meditation brings about *transformation*. Romans 12:2 tells us we are transformed by the renewing of our minds. Changing our mind comes before changing our lives. Meditation enables us to "calm the brain and body and usher the soul into the power, mystery, and sublime presence of the sacred" (3). In that sublime presence, we will be changed. We will become more and more like Jesus, not because we are trying harder, but because we have quieted the other voices in our heads and have learned to listen to His.

Growing in our relationship with God is not adding one more thing to our "to do" list, but, instead, stopping to listen to God who speaks in a quiet whisper. You have been practicing meditation and quietness before God in these weeks and I hope you are beginning to understand its power and benefit in your life.

TUESDAY

MEDITATION

"In repentance and rest is your salvation, in quietness and trust is your strength." (Isaiah 30:15a)

Think about what it means to be quiet before God and what it means to trust in him. Allow this Word of God to sink into your very being. Accept it as truth from God's heart to yours. Write down the thoughts that come to you mind after your time of meditation.

WEDNESDAY

THOUGHTS FOR TODAY

When Paul wrote to his young protégé' he told him to "Reflect on what I am saying, for the Lord will give you insight into all this" (2 Timothy 2:7). As we reflect on God's Word, we are given understanding that we will not have if we simply read through a passage and then go on our way.

The writer of Hebrews tells us that the Word of God is living and active. If we let the words of Scripture take up residence in our hearts through meditation, they come alive to us and begin to change us from the inside out. I make it a practice to ask the Spirit for a verse or a phrase from Scripture every morning. Then, as I go through that day, I ponder the words of the verse and, in doing so, I am filling my mind and heart with the very words of God – living, active and powerful words.

Sometimes we need reminders for, for that, sticky notes are a great spiritual tool! If you choose a verse for your daily meditation, post it in places you will see it: the dashboard of your car, next to your telephone, at your desk, or on your mirror. When you see the note, think of the words, mull them over in your mind, pray them back to God, and let them just live inside of you. Before you realize it, you will begin to be changed by the powerful internalized words of God.

THURSDAY
THOUGHTS FOR TODAY

There are things other than Scripture that we can use as a focus of contemplation as well. Psalm 19:1 tells us that we can see God's glory in the work of His hands. What has God revealed about Himself in creation? In the tiniest of creatures and in the vastness of the heavens? Creation can be a meditative focus that enables us to know and understand God better.

Perhaps our primary focus should be God himself. There are many times in scripture we are told to think in silence about God.

". . . stand in awe of God." (Ecclesiastes 5:7b)

"Be still and know that I am God." (Psalm 46:10)

"I think of you through the watches of the night." (Psalm 63:6)

How much time are we willing to spend just being in awe of God, thinking about His character and His greatness? As we keep ourselves mentally in God's presence and focus on Him, His voice speaks to us internally and His power changes us. We will find that we are compelled to worship as we realize the amazing majesty of God.

I think it is also important for us to meditate on events in our lives and in the world around us. We are told that sometimes things happen as examples for our learning (1 Corinthians 10:6). God sometimes chooses to speak through things that happen, but we have to be still before Him and listen to the message He desires to give.

FRIDAY
READING GOD'S MESSAGE

John 6:1-15

Read this account of the feeding of the 5,000 and, through meditation and imagination, place yourself in the story as one of the characters. Take in the noises, the smells, and the scenery around you. Feel the hunger and witness the miracle. Imagine you are Philip, Andrew, Mary, or one of the crowd and absorb all you can of Jesus, His love, His power, and His character as you participate. Take your time through this process.

What spiritual insights do you gain from this experience?

SATURDAY
FOR PERSONAL REFLECTION

How has your concept of meditation changed as you have participated in *GodSense* meditations so far this year?

Is there a particular kind of contemplation that most effectively takes you into God's presence?

After reading this week's thoughts, is there a new kind of meditation that you would like to try?

Why do you think meditation/contemplation is pleasing to God?

SUNDAY
PRAYER

Lord, you have helped me to go from loneliness to solitude through Your example of going off alone to pray and to be in communion with the Father. Your intimacy with the Father is what I am after. In quietness and confidence is my strength. I melt into Your peace, confident that when I'm with You I have everything I need. I will never be separated from Your love. Let me share this never-ending love with all those I meet today. I will look into eyes and assure them that they are loved by a greater power than I. I will be Your instrument of love, Lord. Just keep growing me into more and more of You. I ask this in Your powerful and holy name. Amen.

    (3) Leonard Sweet, *Soul Salsa: 17 Surprising Steps for Godly Living* (Grand Rapids: Zondervan), 2000.

WEEK EIGHT

Sacred Pauses

"The King, full of mercy and goodness, very far from chastising me, embraces me with love, makes me eat at His table, serves me with His own hands, gives me the key of His treasures; He converses and delights Himself with me incessantly, in a thousand and a thousand ways, and treats me in all respects as His favorite. It is thus I consider myself from time to time in His holy presence."
– Brother Lawrence

MONDAY
THOUGHTS FOR TODAY

Associated with contemplation, as we talked about last week, a practice that has been life-changing for me in the quest for knowing God is called "listening prayer". This is God-focused prayer that invites a two-way conversation with Him. Want to try it? Here are some guidelines that might help:

Greeting: Open the conversation with a greeting that acknowledges God's presence and His power. I often say, "Good morning, Heavenly Father. I worship You as the Creator and Sustainer of the universe." Then I stop to think about Him in his majesty and glory and I praise Him for the creation He has made and all the gifts He gives moment-by-moment.

Surrender: In your own words, invite the Holy Spirit to take over your entire being, to speak to your spirit, and to protect you from the evil one.

Confession: Ask the Spirit to reveal any sins for which you need to repent. Confess as soon as He points them out. Sin will block the voice of God, so you need to make sure the pathway is clear.

Quiet: Try to eliminate distractions. Often, I simply ask myself, "What burdens do I need to lay down?" Then, as they come to mind, I give them over to God to hold while I turn my attention completely to Him.

Ask: If you are wrestling with a problem or sense a need for direction, ask Him a specific question. He has answers you cannot even conceive, but we need to verbalize our need to Him. If you just want to know His presence and rest in His care, tell Him so. He wants to respond to that, too.

Wait: Now pause to listen. God desires that prayer be two-way communication. He speaks continually and we will hear His voice within us if we take time to listen. Because you have prepared your heart and asked for Holy Spirit protection from evil influences, believe that any thought that comes into your mind at this point is from God. Of course, we always test messages against what is revealed in the Bible about God's will and His character, but as you get accustomed to hearing God's voice, you will begin to recognize messages is from Him.

Write: Write it down any message you sense. When God speaks, it's important enough that you don't want to forget it.

Obey: Follow any direction He gives. I have found that God stops speaking if I have chosen not to respond to any previous command He has given me. He speaks so He can direct and change us. Our job is to accept His message by faith and simply do what He says to do.

Praise: You will not be able resist thanking and praising God for His care for you. Amazing things happen in His presence.

TUESDAY
MEDITATION

"You have made known to me the path of life; in your presence there is fullness of joy; at your right hand are pleasures forevermore." (Psalm 16:11 ESV)

Think about these words and, after your meditation, think about all the good you receive from your relationship with God. Write down any thoughts that come to your mind.

WEDNESDAY

THOUGHTS FOR TODAY

Followers of Islam pray five times a day. Jews practice morning, afternoon, and evening prayers. Benedictine monks stop seven times every day for prayer and worship. What about us? I have my morning devotion time, to be sure, but the activity of the day can draw me away from connecting with God unless I intentionally bring myself back to awareness of Him. You, too? God deeply desires for us to be in continual unbroken relationship with Him. It seems He is just waiting for us to respond to His loving invitation.

I'd like to propose a "sacred pause challenge". Most likely our work days or our pace will not allow us to pause *seven* times, but maybe we could make a small adjustment to schedule and pause *one* time in the middle of things to acknowledge our Creator. Here are some ideas of things we could do with a sacred pause:

- Choose a verse from our morning devotional time and reread it a few times aloud.
- Thank God for at least three things.
- Praise God for at least three of His attributes.
- Sing Him a song.
- Take a few deep breaths, quieting the body and mind, then just be still before Him.

Once we develop the habit of a midday sacred pause, we could add another and another until we are in touch with God throughout our day – every day. He will be pleased and we will be blessed!

THURSDAY

THOUGHTS FOR TODAY

We have talked quite a bit so far about listening for God's voice. But the other side of prayer – the talking side – is important, too. I believe God wants the kind of relationship with us that Jesus had with His disciples. The kind where we walk together, talking as we go.

One day I was taking my two young grandchildren to the local library. On the way, the one-year old was riding contentedly in his car seat and the three-year old was in her adjacent seat, saying something that I couldn't understand. I had tuned her out due to traffic concerns, but, after a minute, I turned and said, "I didn't hear you, honey, can you tell me what you were saying?"

"I wasn't talking to you," she responded. "I was talking to God."

"Oh, you were PRAYING."

"No, I was just talking to Him."

She was three years old and understood something I had been trying to put my finger on for years. God wants the kind of relationship with me where there is continual conversation. I am learning, yet, to talk to Him as I go through my day. To remember that He is always present and always eager to have His presence acknowledged and enjoyed. I can't say that I pray all day long, but often I do find myself ". . . just talking to Him." Do you, too?

The Bible tells us ". . . the eyes of the Lord are on the righteous and His ears are attentive to their prayer." (1 Peter 3:12). He is just waiting for us to begin the conversation – anytime, anywhere.

FRIDAY
READING GOD'S MESSAGE

Prayer Promises

Write the promise given in each of these verses on prayer:

Psalm 16:8

Isaiah 64:4

Jeremiah 33:3

Luke 1:37

John 14:12-14

Philippians 4:19

How do these promises provide encouragement for you to be more focused on a life of prayer?

SATURDAY
FOR PERSONAL REFLECTION

As you think about what we have learned this week about developing a conversational relationship with God, what do you commit to changing about your prayer life? Why?

When you listen for God's direction in prayer, how do you know it is His voice? How do you think you can develop ways to learn to recognize His voice?

How do you respond when God speaks to you in your thoughts?

What practices can you build into your day that will help you grow a greater awareness of God's presence in your life?

SUNDAY
PRAYER

"Sacred is the pause that draws us into stillness. Nourishing are the moments when we step away from busyness. Teach us the wisdom of pausing. Reveal to us the goodness of stopping to breathe. Bring to our memory the truth that we are the temple out of which You pour Your gifts into the world. We are the temple from which You sing Your songs. We are the temple out of which You bless. Enable us to listen to the renewal You are trying to bring about in us and through us". (4)

(4) Macrina Weiderkehr, *Seven Sacred Pauses: Living Mindfully Through the Hours of the Day* (Notre Dame, Indiana: Sorin Books, 2008), p. 82

WEEK NINE

Adopted into God's Family

"Define yourself radically as one beloved by God. This is the true self. Every other identity is illusion." – Brennan Manning

MONDAY

THOUGHTS FOR TODAY

In these past few weeks, we have learned about God's love and have talked about ways we can connect with Him on a heart level. We are beginning to realize what a great blessing it is to be part of His eternal family. Over the next few weeks, we will explore ways God treats us as His beloved children. Let's begin.

We are all needy human beings. We are born into this world as helpless creatures relying on others to meet our every need. "This (family) is the nest in which soul is born, nurtured, and released into life. . . "(5). Since the role of our original family is so critical in our development, let's think for a moment about how we would describe the perfect parent. Here are some things that come immediately to my mind. A good parent . . .

is present in our lives, is available to us.
is loving and cares about us as individuals within the family.
provides for our needs.
protects us and makes us feel secure.
is interested in us and in what we do.
plays with us.
is wise in guiding us.
trains and teaches us.
disciplines us.
desires the best for us.
helps us to grow up to become contributing members of society.

Were your parents like that? Perhaps in many ways they were, but even a very good parent will fall short. Perfection is not attainable in this life. But, as human beings, we still have the need for parenting like that. Are those needs forever to go unmet, or to be met only in part? No. There is a solution. The distresses we have in this life because our original families were not perfect can be overcome. The hurts inflicted by authority figures can be soothed and the emotional scars left by inadequate family modeling can be effectively remedied.

What is the solution? Taking God up on His offer to adopt us into His eternal family. He becomes our perfect heavenly parent and completely and eternally fills every need we have. We will look at the details of this too-good-to-be-true offer as we walk together this week.

TUESDAY

MEDITATION

"God's Spirit touches our spirits and confirms who we really are. We know who he is, and we know who we are: Father and children." (Romans 8:14-15 *The Message*)

As you meditate on these words, allow the Spirit of God to confirm that you are God's specially loved and chosen child. Write down any thoughts that come to your mind.

WEDNESDAY

THOUGHTS FOR TODAY

When God creates a need, He has a plan for fulfillment of that need. He created thirst and gives us water to quench the thirst. He created hunger and gives us good food to fill the hunger. He created us with a desire for significance and has given us work to do which helps to satisfy that desire. He created us with a longing for immortality and provides eternal life to fulfill that longing. God, in His great wholeness, never creates a need He will not fill. He is both the starter and the finisher of all that He creates.

If He begins something, He completes it. Therefore, we can believe that if He put within our hearts the need for nurturing or the desire to belong to a loving family, He has also made a way to completely satisfy that longing. As we grow in our spiritual awareness, we recognize that all the ideals of parenthood are met in our heavenly Father, whom Jesus called "Abba", roughly translated "Daddy". Our relationship with Him will fill all the empty places in our lives left by even the best of earthly relationships. God has a solution to the pains we feel as a result of lacks in our human relationships. After all, He built the need into us in the first place. Now we find that He is willing to be the one to fill it. In fact, He is the only one who *can*.

THURSDAY
THOUGHTS FOR TODAY

Adam and Eve's fall into sin did not take God by surprise. But He never intended that they should remain separated from Him by the choice they had made. So, before He even made this world, God had a plan to deliver fallen man from Satan, the enemy of God and of us as humans. That loving rescue plan included not only Adam and Eve, but also those of us who would acknowledge and accept the price that He paid and, through that acceptance, become part of His eternal family.

The ability for us to become children of God originates in God's grace. His choice to make us His children was made before we ever came into being. Our acceptance into His family is not dependent upon our worthiness or our goodness. Our position as sons or daughters of God rests on the everlasting love of God. It should give us great comfort to know that our acceptance by God is not tied to our having to measure up. We can stop trying so hard. We can simply accept with gratefulness the fact that we are loved and we belong.

Eventually we will find that the only fulfillment to the drive to belong comes from our relationship with our heavenly Father and with others who belong to Him, too. He invites us to belong. His family is not complete without all of his specially selected children. Once we are His, we belong to Him forever. We will always fit in.

FRIDAY
READING GOD'S MESSAGE

Ephesians 1:3-14

What do verses 5 and 9 tell us about how God feels about having us in His family?

How do verses 7 and 8 enable us to meet the family requirements given in verse 4?

Who is to be most honored by our being in the family of God? (v. 12)

What does the Holy Spirit guarantee that we will someday receive? (v. 14)

What do you think that inheritance will be?

SATURDAY
FOR PERSONAL REFLECTION

What are some of the basic needs that we are born with as human beings?

What are some of the things that keep parents from being able to meet those needs for their children?

How can knowledge of the fact that our eternal Father fills our deepest needs be of comfort to those of us who recognize our own failing as earthly parents?

How did you become God's child? What would you say to someone who asked you how he or she could become part of God's family?

SUNDAY
PRAYER

Lord, I will praise you no matter what happens or no matter what has happened to me. Everything that does not praise you is ruled out of my life in your name, Jesus. Today I choose to focus on letting myself be transformed into Your image. Let these circumstances of life be an opportunity to grow closer to You, Holy Spirit, my breath of life. Continue to breathe into me the joy of Your holiness. Bring me back from gray exile, put a fresh wind in my sails! Praise be to you, O God! Amen.

(5) Thomas More, *Care of the Soul*, (New York: Harper Perennial, 1995) pp. 28-29

WEEK TEN

Meeting Us in Our Need

"He gives us what we need even when we don't feel like it's enough, and our acceptance is good practice in surrender." – Angie Smith

MONDAY
THOUGHTS FOR TODAY

God knows that, in His family, when it comes to providing for ourselves, we are but babies. We depend 100% on His provision for us. God likes it that way. He encourages us to rely on Him and promises to provide for us. Jesus tells us to ask, seek, and knock and we will be given, we will find, and the door will be opened. Then He goes on to illustrate this by saying that if your child asks you for a piece of bread (maybe pizza in today's world!), will you give him a stone? Or if asks for a fish, will give him a snake instead? No, you will try as a parent to meet the child's needs and, whenever possible and when you think it is in his best interest, you will try to meet his wants as well.

God is like that, too, Jesus says. In fact, He does it better. Jesus says, "If you, then, though you are evil, know how to give good gifts to your children, how much more will your Father in heaven give good gifts to those who ask him!" (Matthew 7:11). In His loving goodness, God wants to provide for us and when we have needs, He expects us to call on Him for that provision. Our role is to acknowledge that everything we have comes from God who desires to give us good gifts and then to accept with thanksgiving all that He graciously gives us.

We can ask in confidence knowing that God has no limitations as our provider. He is not short on resources. The Bible tells us that everything under heaven belongs to Him (Job 41:11). Economic recessions don't cause a moment's worry for God. Predicted overpopulation and resultant food shortages don't make Him sweat even a little. If all that is on the earth belongs to God, then it is His to distribute as He wishes. He can reverse famines. He can supernaturally supply food, shelter, and other needs for His children. Remember He sent ravens to deliver food to Elijah when he was hungry in the wilderness. He sent manna for the people of Israel when they were wandering in the desert. Jesus multiplied bread and fish to feed 5,000 plus people who had listened all day to His teaching.

There are no limitations to what God can provide if He so chooses. But He does want us to ask.

TUESDAY

MEDITATION

"Now, there is great gain in godliness with contentment." (1 Timothy 6:6 *ESV*)

Meditate on the words of this teaching and allow God to speak to you through it. Write down any thoughts that come into your mind.

WEDNESDAY

THOUGHTS FOR TODAY

Of far greater significant than the materials things God provides for us on a day-by-day basis, is the life-giving provision He has made for us to have a love relationship with Him both now and throughout eternity. Remember when Jesus sent out the disciples two-by-two to work miracles and spread the news that the Messiah had come? When they returned from that excursion, they excitedly reported back to Him how they were able to heal the sick and cast out demons. That was a real high for these common Galileans!

But Jesus brought everything into perspective when He said, " . . . do not rejoice that the spirits submit to you, but rejoice that your names are written I heaven." (Luke 10:20). He was telling that to keep an eternal perspective. The things happening around them here on earth were exciting, to be sure, but if they really wanted to know what was important, they needed to look ahead to the fact that they would live forever in heaven with God.

Today, Jesus might say to us, "Do not rejoice that you have two cars in your garage, you were promoted at work, or the mortgage has been paid off, but rejoice that your name is written in heaven." God has seen the real needs of our hearts and has made the ultimate provision to fulfill those needs. We need Him. We need His forgiveness, and we need a vital relationship with Him. God has provided all that!

THURSDAY
THOUGHTS FOR TODAY

When we learn to depend on God and not on ourselves, there are godly characteristics that will begin to show up in our lives. Let's take a look.

Honesty. There is no need to cheat on our income taxes, to put a spin on our loan applications, or to overcharge in our businesses if God is our provider. We are responsible only to be good trustees of what He gives, conducting ourselves in honesty and fairness.

Confidence. When we give God priority status in our lives, He provides for us, and we can quit worrying. Such a confident lifestyle immediately elevates our eyes. Instead of looking around us at the things that we need or want, we look up to God, knowing He will provide everything that is good in His perfect timing.

Gratefulness. We can choose to focus on the graciousness of our heavenly provider, or we can, like the Israelites, complain that we are bored with manna. Choosing an attitude of thanksgiving will create joy in our hearts.

Generosity. If we acknowledge that everything we have comes from God, we will be eager to share what we have with those in need around us. Our spiritual growth is not complete until we have learned to give.

Eternal focus. Whatever possessions or wealth we have when we die will remain here. All of it. How wise we are if we live for eternity that has no end instead of for this life which lasts but a moment and then is gone.

FRIDAY

READING GOD'S MESSAGE

Matthew 6:19-21

Where are we not to store up treasure? Why?

Where should we be storing up treasures? Why are they safer there?

What do you think Jesus means by "treasures" in these verses?

How is your heart (your emotions) a way to measure where your treasure is?

What does your heart tell you about any adjustment in focus you need to make between earthly treasures and heavenly treasures? Are you willing to make that adjustment?

SATURDAY
FOR PERSONAL REFLECTION

Spend some time with God in prayer asking Him the following questions:

What things, people, or activities have become my treasures?

Which of those are building treasures of eternal value?

Which of those do You want me to give less attention to? Why?

Which do You want me to focus more attention on? How?
Tell God that you will trust Him to be your provider so you can be more focused on eternity's values.

SUNDAY
PRAYER

Holy Spirit, I want Your fruit living in me; You are the way that I choose to go, showing everyone around me love, joy, gentleness, peace, kindness, patience, faithfulness, goodness and self-control. Bind me to Your spirit, Soul of my soul, and never let me go. In You there is fullness of joy and pleasures forevermore. This is what I really desire. Help me to let everything else go so I can receive more of You. My hands are open. I will praise You so long as there is breath in me. Hallelujah to the King!

WEEK ELEVEN

Family Forever

"The beauty of heaven is seeing God." – Max Lucado

MONDAY

THOUGHTS FOR TODAY

Comedian George Carlin once quipped, "I'm always relieved when someone delivers a eulogy and I realize I'm listening to it." Most of us feel that way. We want to live and to hang onto the familiarity of the life that we know. Even if it is not a perfect existence, we cling to it because this body is how we know ourselves, it is how we relate to people, it is how we are identified, it holds who we are.

The real security of being in God's family is that it is not just for life on earth, but it is a relationship that will last forever. We, rightfully, place great value on this physical life because we realize it will end someday, at least in the form that we now know and experience it. Knowing that there are limits to the length of this life gives us an urgency to be, to become, to do, to plan, to relate, and, overall, to infuse our lives with meaning. Life is a gift, it is of limited duration, and we know instinctively that it has great value.

Jesus, as God in a physical body, valued human life more than any of us ever could. He raised the dead, He comforted the mourners, and He pointed to a future that would exist someday without being overshadowed by an eventual death. Jesus entered this world of time and mortality partly to let us know that this earthly life is only a foreshadowing of the real and everlasting life that is yet to come. He taught us that the life we live will change, but it will never end. We are eternal beings who are temporarily residing on earth in its present state and, although we will pass through a transition called death, we will live forever. Jesus wants that forever to be spent with Him.

Before Jesus came to earth, scholars and religious leaders tried to figure out life beyond the grave by studying the Old Testament scriptures. One day, Jesus looked them in the eye and told them that when the scriptures spoke about eternal life, those words were pointing to Him (John 5:39). He was the answer to humankind's search for life that never ends. The Old Testament writers had given a hint that there would be a resurrection of our bodies though they had died; that we would experience unending life in some form, in some place; and that there exists a life outside of the realm of time which was known. But Jesus came to tell us about that life and to invite us to participate in His eternal plan for us.

TUESDAY

MEDITATION

"Now this is eternal life: that they may know you, the only true God, and Jesus Christ, whom you have sent." (John 17:3)

Meditate on the words of this verse and allow the Spirit to open your understanding of eternal life. Write down any thoughts that come to your mind.

WEDNESDAY

THOUGHTS FOR TODAY

The best-known verse in the Bible is the one in which Jesus revealed that He is the means by whom never-ending life is provided, "For God so loved the world that he gave his one and only Son, that whoever believes in him shall not perish but have eternal life." (John 3:16). Once this gift of life is given, we have eternity springing up in us. We have a sense of forever, of meaning, and of purpose that goes way beyond the routines in which we engage day-by-day.

Jesus lived as God among us for thirty-some years and he was not oblivious to the fact that human creatures fear death. His own impending death and the sin bearing related to it caused Him great sorrow as He prayed in the garden. Eternal life begins within us, but Jesus recognized that there is a dread of the transition from earthly life to heavenly life. Jesus compared death to a seed being planted into the ground. By dying to being a seed, it eventually grows into a productive and beautiful plant.

Just so, when we mortals die to the confines of physical life, the eternal life that was hidden within us as a seed sprouts to a new existence. The eternal life we have by knowing Jesus has only limited opportunity to manifest itself while we are bound to our present bodies. Death bursts the limitations of this life and frees us to enter the world of forever becoming.

THURSDAY

THOUGHTS FOR TODAY

Jesus told His followers that, although He was about to leave them physically, He was going to prepare a place for them so that someday He and they could be together again. They would be separated for a while, but eventually He would take them home with Him forever. That promise is for us, too.

I wonder what kind of place Jesus is preparing for us. The Bible gives us glimpses of heaven, but only glimpses because we are told that the real thing is simply not describable! But we do see that there will be gold, jewels, peace, plenty, and conversation. The deepest needs of our heart will be met as we are healed emotionally and become whole. Sin will be left outside the door so we no longer will struggle with temptation and failure. We will be overwhelmed with love that we give and receive and, therefore, all sense of comparison and competition with one another is gone. And most of all, we will be acutely and joyfully aware of the loving presence of God. As we worship Him and walk with Jesus we will find that nothing blocks our oneness with Him. In the perfect place Jesus is preparing for us, we will, at last and for always, be home.

Eternal life is God himself, not just something He passes out to us. He gives us Himself and in that gift, awakens in us real life in His family that begins now and lasts forever.

FRIDAY

READING GOD'S MESSAGE

John 14:1-4

Read this passage through two or three times, thinking about its significance (it might be helpful to read it in more than one version

Then answer these questions:

What does Jesus tell us to do instead of being troubled or anxious?

Why is trusting God and trusting Jesus the same thing?

What Jesus refers to His Father's house, what is He talking about?

What does Jesus promise He is doing for us in His Father's house?

What does Jesus promise to come back to do?

How do you feel when you think about Jesus wanting us to be with Him forever?

SATURDAY
FOR PERSONAL REFLECTION

What longings do you have that are not being completely fulfilled in this life?

Where do you think those desires came from?

How does just having those longings increase your faith?

In what ways can you structure your life in this world to respond to those desires?

Spend some time in prayer, committing yourself to God and asking Him to fill you with longings that draw you closer to Him. Sense His love for you and accept the peace with which He fills your heart. Write down any thoughts you have as you pause to listen for God's response.

SUNDAY
PRAYER

O God of Truth, fill me with Your truth; for me truth no longer is a factor, it is a person. It is you, O Jesus, O Jesus. Have mercy on me and grant me Your truth so that in all areas of my life, I may walk in Truth, that I may walk in Jesus. I want to live so close to you that when You take a step, I follow. I will follow you right to the Father's house where there is rejoicing always. Let me practice this rejoicing now. Only in your energy, Holy Spirit will this be possible. You are my pressing necessity. I pray in your holy name. Amen.

WEEK TWELVE

Knowing God, Knowing Ourselves

"Nothing except our reluctance prevents us from enjoying the intimacy of this union. The dividing wall has been broken down and we are free to seek our fill of God's presence." – Calvin Miller

MONDAY

THOUGHTS FOR TODAY

Do you know how it feels to be in love? You sense that your lover knows everything about you, understands you as no one else on earth does, and loves you unconditionally. Think long phone calls, constant texting, in-depth conversations at Starbucks, lengthy good-byes at the end of the day, and the reluctance to be apart for even a few hours. You want to know this person and to be known by him or her in return. You desire intimacy. The longing for intimacy is a God-given longing that He desires to fill. The desire for closeness and understanding is a healthy one that has been implanted in us by our Father in Heaven. Knowing that intimacy is part of God's plan for us, how do we nurture relationships that will fill our yearning for that kind of oneness?

On a human level, developing this kind of relationship takes two fundamental things: time and truth. Part of becoming intimate with another human being is being willing to spend enough time together. True intimacy develops over a period of years as people are committed to standing with one another through all the revelations, struggles, pains, and joys of life. That is why marriage is the example God gives us of a truly intimate relationship. And that is why falling in love feels so good. We sense that at last we have found someone who truly understands us!

But time without truth will not build intimacy. We will never get to know the real person underneath the facades (and we all have them) until we are able to break through to truth about ourselves and truth about the person with whom we are in relationship. It takes two whole, honest, committed people to develop the kind of intimacy that will begin to fill the longing in our hearts. The lack of commitment of time over the long haul and the lack of honesty often combine to create disappointments as we realize that, although human relationships bring a certain amount of happiness, they cannot satisfy entirely the deepest longings of our hearts.

While God desires for us to develop intimate human relationships, He knows that our need for true and complete intimacy will be fulfilled only in relationship with Him. He believes we are worth knowing. He will listen to us without ever growing tired. And He wants us to know Him, too. He is ready to be found and to be enjoyed.

TUESDAY

MEDITATION

"We'll see it all then, see it all as clearly as God sees us, knowing him directly just as he knows us!" (1 Corinthians 13:12b *The Message)*

Think about the words of this verse, pondering God's intimate knowledge of you and on His revelation of Himself to you that is growing day by day until someday you will know Him as well as He knows you now. Write down any thoughts that you may have after you spend your time in meditation.

WEDNESDAY

THOUGHTS FOR TODAY

How intimately does God already know us? The psalm writer says, ". . . his understanding has no limit" (Psalm 147:5b). There is nothing that He does not know about us. He is not surprised by anything, He does not have to learn anything or acquire new knowledge, and His knowledge transcends time. In other words, He knows everything there is to know about our past, present, and future. We can't surprise Him!

God is present with us and knows everything we do and think, have done and have thought, and will do and will think. It will never come as a shock to Him when our true motives are revealed or our actions don't measure up even to our own expectations of ourselves. He knows and He loves us anyway.

But, God not only knows everything about us Himself, He also takes the time to show *us* the truth about ourselves. And that knowledge is beyond any that we could ever know by our own efforts. It is a gift of revelation that God gives to those who yield to Him, spend time with Him, and humbly wait for Him to uncover truth. The more we become aware of His presence in our lives and the more we recognize His awareness of all there is to know about us, the more honestly we can deal with our failures and the more confidently we can acknowledge our God-given strengths. He helps us to know and understand ourselves so we can relate to Him in truth.

THURSDAY

THOUGHTS FOR TODAY

The amazing thing about our relationship with God is not just that He knows us, but that, over time, He allows us to know Him. He wants us eventually to know Him just as completely, just as intimately, as He knows us. He created us for intimacy and He will see to it that intimacy between us and Him really does happen. We have already read the promise He gives, ". . . now I know in part; then I shall know fully, even as I am fully known (1 Corinthians 13:12b). In this world we know God in limited ways. We read His word, we see His revelation in nature and in people around us, and we pray, allowing Him to reveal Himself and His will to us. This is experiential, growing, developing knowledge. But it is an incomplete knowing (". . . now I know in part").

We are told, though, that the day will come when ". . . I shall know fully, even as I am fully known." This is a full, clear, thorough knowledge. This is 100% intimacy. We are promised that someday all our faltering steps of obedience, understanding, and reaching out toward God will be behind us and our knowledge and relationship will be complete and perfect. Our desires for intimacy on this earth are partially met in relationships with other people and more completely met in our relationship with God, but they will be fully met only when we see Him face-to-face.

FRIDAY

READING GOD'S MESSAGE

John 13:36-38; Acts 2:36-41

What claim did Peter make about his loyalty to Jesus?

What did Jesus say that showed that He knew Peter better than Peter knew himself?

Who was right? (If you are not sure, check out John 18)

Do you think Jesus loved Peter less because He knew Peter would deny him? Why or why not?

In Acts, we read a powerful message that Peter is giving to the Jews in Jerusalem. How had Peter's personality changed since his cowardly denials at the time of Jesus' arrest?

To what do you attribute that change?

What does this tell us about the effect in our lives of God's intimate knowledge of us?

SATURDAY
FOR PERSONAL REFLECTION

Write down the names of two or three people in your life with whom you experience the most intimacy. Think of ways to show them this week how much you appreciate their friendship.

Are there any close personal relationships in which you need to be more truthful? Or to which you need to commit more time? If so, think about ways you can develop deeper intimacy.

What are some ways in which we can get to know God better? What is your favorite way? What other way(s) are you willing to try so you can increase your intimacy with Him?

SUNDAY

PRAYER

Lord, you are the God of time; my time is in Your hands. That is the only safe place for me to be. You say in your Word, Lord, that I am engraved on the palm of Your hand. Nothing can separate me from Your love. This is my security, this is my assurance that no matter where I go, where life takes me, what circumstances surround me, You are there holding me with Your powerful hands, loving me with Your powerful love. My security is in knowing that I have Your non-separating, all-powerful love all the time. It is an eternal supply. I am grateful and my heart overflows with love back to You. Help me to stay in this flow of love. I ask all this in Jesus' loving name. Amen

WEEK THIRTEEN

Experiencing Unconditional Love

"We should be astonished at the goodness of God, stunned that He should bother to call us by name, our mouths wide open at His love, bewildered that at this very moment we are standing on holy ground.
– Brennan Manning

MONDAY

THOUGHTS FOR TODAY

Earthly fathers love their children, but there is no love like the love we receive from our Father in Heaven.

True love has been defined by M. Scott Peck as an act of the will, a decision to move into relationship with another human being, in most part, for the benefit of the one who is loved and often at the expense of the one who loves (6). Real love is a choice and it is a choice to put another ahead of yourself. That kind of love does occur in human experience, but it seems to be the love that we are able to give only after we have matured, have gained some sense of our own being, and have enough of our own needs met emotionally so that we are able to look beyond ourselves to the needs and desires of another person. Even then, we can love only imperfectly.

As we look at Scripture, we realize that the definition of authentic love that Peck gives us is the *only* way that God loves. First, His love for us is a choice. Ephesians 1:4 tells us that God chose us before the creation of the world, in love, to be adopted into His family. God did not accidentally fall in love with us.

Second, His choice to love us cost Him something. In fact, it cost the entering of Jesus into this world to redeem us.

Third, His love for us is for our benefit. God's loving choice was not based upon His own need. He was not lonely as some pseudo-theologians would have us think. God lacks nothing. He has fellowship within the Trinity that is far deeper than any fellowship that He could have with humans, but He chose to create us anyway and, He, further, chose to love and adopt us as His children. God loves us as we are, then invites us to grow up into Him, to know Him, and to become, by His grace, just like Jesus Christ.

God's choosing us, growing us, guiding us, and ultimately making us like Him fit perfectly the definition of true love.

Throughout the Bible we see that God created us to bring glory to Himself because He alone is deserving of praise, worship, and adoration. As we offer Him that glory and praise, we participate in His love, and we enjoy Him. That was why God created us: So we could enjoy each other forever. Perfect love brings perfect joy.

TUESDAY

MEDITATION

". . . if we love one another, God dwells deeply within us, and his love becomes complete in us – perfect love! (1 John 4:12 *The Message*)

Meditate on this verse and allow God to fill you up with His perfect love. Thank Him. Write down any thoughts you have when you have completed your time of meditation.

WEDNESDAY

THOUGHTS FOR TODAY

As we read the Bible, we begin to understand that we do not have to convince God to love us. His love is freely, fully, and unconditionally given. It is important for us to remember that God is both the initiator and the sustainer of this intimate relationship He has with us. In our humanness, we will fail to live up to our own expectations of our role in this relationship. We will sin, we will not feel so close to God at times, and we will sometimes reject Him. When we do, we will think that God cannot possibly love us, that we are unworthy, and that He really doesn't want us to be close. But we will be wrong about that!

In reality, God's love for us is not dependent upon our lovability (there are days I am really glad about that!). It is entirely based upon God's commitment to us. He made the choice from eternity past to love us and that choice will carry us into all the eternity that is yet ahead. Nothing we can do for good or for bad will change that. God's love is the constant. Once we become His children, we can draw closer or pull away, but His love for us will not depend on our response or on our behavior. The interesting psychology of this relationship is that the more we realize how much He loves us, the more that love draws us toward Him and we cannot help responding. His love becomes irresistible!

THURSDAY
THOUGHTS FOR TODAY

While the giving of love is initiated by God, the receiving is the part that, with God's help, is up to us. God wants us to experience His unconditional love in a way that is greater than knowing about Him or knowing His Word; it is a knowledge that comes from experiencing relationship with Him, from walking with Him, and from trusting Him enough to allow Him to fully possess us. That journey results in a knowledge that grows out of communicating with Him, an intimate knowledge that develops only through a love relationship. God sends His love, we simply need to prepare our minds, our emotions, and our wills to open wide and receive it.

Our relationship with Him will fulfill us to a far greater degree than any human love relationship we can imagine. Read it this way from Emilie Griffin, "In this intimacy, in this full dependency and closeness there is freedom, the only freedom we are likely to taste here and now. It is a freedom that comes about not from doing, but from undoing: letting go of all the support systems that sustained us, or seemed to sustain us, before now . . . I love you, I say, but I do not need you to tell me who I am. For the Lord Himself does that, when He whispers His love in my ear every day." (7) . God loves us just because we are His and, by receiving that love, we learn to love Him back.

FRIDAY
READING GOD'S MESSAGE

Ephesians 3:14-21

What does Paul pray for the Christians in verse 16?

What do you think Paul means by being "rooted and established in love"?

What is it that Paul wants his readers to fully understand? (v. 18)

How do you suppose we can "know" a love that "surpasses knowledge" as Paul describes in v. 19?

What should be filling us? (v. 19)

SATURDAY
FOR PERSONAL REFLECTION

Do you ever feel unlovable? At what times or in what circumstances?

How can experiencing the unconditional love of God help you to overcome those feelings?

How does a practice of the spiritual disciplines such as prayer, study, meditation and worship help us to connect to the love that God is sending our way?

Which of the practices listed in the previous question might you try anew this week to enable your love relationship with God to grow deeper?

How does experiencing God's love enable you to show His love to others around you? Is there anyone you need to reach out to in love this week?

SUNDAY
PRAYER

Lord, I confess that I have been afraid of Your love. Such purity is so foreign to me. When I catch a glimpse of it, I want to run from it. Give me understanding of the darkness that is in me and remove this fear of perfect love. Could it be that I am afraid that this love demands my soul, my life, my all? Thank You for allowing me to sit with this while You do the changing. Thank you for giving me Your grace to take one step in submitting to this love. You will not force it, but wait on me to be ready. I love You for Your understanding of this Your mixed-up child. Hold me close. Amen

    (6) M. Scott Peck, *The Road Less Traveled* (New York: Touchstone Publishing, 1988), pp. 81-83.
    (7) Emilie Griffin, *Clinging*, (Wichita, Kansas: Eighth Day Press, 2003), p. 88

WEEK FOURTEEN

No Fear: Protected!

"Here is the world. Beautiful and terrible things will happen. Don't be afraid." – Frederick Buechner

MONDAY

THOUGHTS FOR TODAY

We have good reason these days to have fears for our physical safety:
- Crime rates are high.
- War seems always to be threatening or occurring in some area of the world.
- Traffic deaths and road rage are on the rise.
- Cholesterol, extra pounds, and sedentary lifestyles seem to be new enemies.
- Cancer crops up in our bodies or in the body of someone we love.
- Environmental issues threaten our planet: ozone layer, pollution, population explosion, deforestation, global warming, and so on.

We have fears for our emotional safety:
- One who has committed to love us for the rest of our life, finds someone else instead.
- Children reject our caring commitment to them and go their own way.
- Criticisms, contradictions, and put downs come from our peers.
- Protection seems to be found only in isolation and behind false fronts and thick skins.

We have fears for our spiritual safety:
- Maybe God doesn't exist after all.
- How could God love us when we fall away so often? We think that by now He has surely changed His mind about

wanting us.
- Satan and his demons are our enemies and we feel powerless against them.
- What will happen after we die?

Safety and security are fundamental human needs. When we feel unsafe, we are fearful, and *when* we are afraid, we cannot be the productive, happy, fulfilled people God intends for us to be. So, He, as our all-powerful heavenly Father, offers to protect us, to shield us from attack, and to make sure we have a safe place in which to know and serve Him.

Once we understand that we are protected, that we are safe, and that we are guarded from everything that can cause us eternal harm, we approach our lives and the troubles we face with a new perspective and with total trust in God who loves and cares for us. We can trade our anxieties for peace, our fear for love, our insecurity for confidence. When we are at peace, our bodies heal faster and better, we can rest in the care of our heavenly Father and not be at war with the trials that come into our lives, and we can connect at gut level with God, our Creator. When that occurs (and it can!), we know we need ask for nothing more.

TUESDAY

MEDITATION

"People with their minds set on you, you keep completely whole. Steady on their feet, because they keep at it and don't quit. Depend on God and keep at it because in the Lord God you have a sure thing." (Isaiah 26:3-4 *The Message*)

Read these verses a few times and then focus on a phrase that seems particularly significant to you. Spend a few minutes meditating on that phrase and then write down any thoughts that come to you.

WEDNESDAY

THOUGHTS FOR TODAY

We read in scripture that God offers to protect us when we call upon call upon Him. He even provides angels to guard us! In that case, it seems then that all of us who believe would live to a ripe old age and would never suffer any kind of physical harm. But, as we look around us, we realize that Christians do not seem to live charmed lives. They get sick, they have car accidents, they are robbed and attacked by others, and they die, sometimes at a very young age. How do we reconcile what we know of reality with God's promises of protection?

First, we remember that God's plan is bigger than our problem. There are times when He knows it is better for us to experience some of the difficulties of this life so that, through them, we can learn to trust Him and to know Him better.

Second, we realize that God does not always choose to reverse the effects of evil in this world (not yet, at least) and we, as His children, are susceptible to the results of the fall just as the rest of the world is. Those things include sickness, conflict, death, suffering, and danger.

Third, God's protection of us has an eternal point of view. He heals our true sickness, which is in our hearts. He keeps us from the evil one who would take our souls, not just our bodies. And he assures us a place in heaven where we will experience peace and security forever.

THURSDAY

THOUGHTS FOR TODAY

I remember Ruth, a godly woman in my church and who was sick with cancer. Elders prayed over her, she was anointed with oil, and the entire church pled with God for many months for her recovery. I will never forget the Sunday night when she stood behind the pulpit, after yet another round of treatment, to state boldly and with obvious joy, "I have been healed!" There was an audible catching of breaths throughout the sanctuary and then she went on with her face beaming.

"Oh," she said, "I still have cancer, but an even greater healing has taken place inside me. I am whole spiritually; I am so close to God that I cannot wait to see Him. And do you know what? I would not trade what God has given me now for a new and healthy body. God has healed my heart and my soul. I can experience no greater healing than this."

A few weeks later, Ruth was at home with her heavenly Father. I remember many people in the congregation being disappointed that the healing God gave was "only" spiritual. But, I heard Ruth's heart that night and I believed her when she said that the internal healing she experienced was more real and more significant to her than any physical healing could ever be. Her testimony has never left me because it spoke such a great truth: The help we don't know we need is often greater than the help we ask for.

FRIDAY
READING GOD'S MESSAGE

Matthew 9:1-8

What did the people expect Jesus to do when they brought the paralyzed man to him?

What did Jesus actually say to the man on the mat?

What was the reaction of the people to Jesus' statement?

What kind of healing was more important to Jesus – physical or spiritual?

What does this story teach us about trusting God to meet our needs in answer to our prayers?

SATURDAY
FOR PERSONAL REFLECTION

Make a list of any fears you may have concerning your physical safety, your health, or your emotional security.

Present your list to God, asking that He meet the deepest needs of your heart.

Thank Him for caring enough to meet the needs you have that you may not even know about.

Commit your life into His hands, trusting His great love and unlimited power to keep you safe.

SUNDAY
PRAYER

My Father, perfect peace is Your promise and my mind being focused on You is the condition. Is it possible for my mind to be focused on You? Today I pray for grace to quiet my mind so I can hear Your voice, Holy Spirit, as it speaks to my spirit. As I listen to that still, small voice, my whole organism is quieted. You are an awesome God to do this for me. What kind of love is this, O my soul? Through this love You are training me, Your child, to keep my mind steadfast and my trust in You strong and healthy. This is the kind of health I desire. Thank you, Father, that You will give me the desires of my heart as I delight myself in You. How fun! Glory be to You, O Christ! Amen.

WEEK FIFTEEN

Taught by the Great Teacher

"Every happening, great and small, is a parable whereby God speaks to us, and the art of life is to get the message." – Malcolm Muggeridge

MONDAY

THOUGHTS FOR TODAY

    The Bible tells of a conversation Moses and God had many years ago (Exodus 33:13-21). Moses had been commissioned by God to lead the Israelites out of their slavery in Egypt into the freedom of the land God had promised them. At this point in the story they have been miraculously taken out from slavery under Pharaoh, have crossed the Red Sea which parted for them, and are at their first stop in the desert: Mount Sinai. Here they set up camp for a while so that God can communicate to Moses the law which would govern the people's morality, their government, and their worship. It seems that the more time Moses and God spent together, the greater Moses' desire grew to know God more completely. Finally, Moses said to God, "If you are pleased with me, teach me your ways so I may know you …"

    Moses courageously and humbly invited God to teach him. And what reasons did he give for being open to the teaching God would give? ". . . so I may know You. . ." God knows us inside and out. He knows what we think and what we will do before we do it. He ordained the day we were born and knows the day we will die. He knows what drives us and what eats at us. He knows how to make us smile and what will make us cry.

    What do we know about God? Sometimes it feels as if we know a lot through the revelation He has given of Himself in the Bible, in creation, in Jesus, and through the Holy Spirit. At other times, we realize how little we know and the best prayer we can pray is the one that Moses prayed, ". . . teach me your ways so I may know you . . ."

    From Moses we learn that our motivation in asking God to teach us must be that we may know Him better. There are many who are driven to knowledge of God so they can claim miracles, they can quote passages of scripture, or they can tell stories about how God has given them special insights. Such motivation is self-serving, arrogant, and sensational. God will not teach those who do not approach Him in humility and in sincerity of heart throwing everything else aside to know Him only. There is nothing more important that the simple goal of knowing God. And we grow to know Him by allowing Him to teach us who He is.

TUESDAY
MEDITATION

"I will give them a heart to know me, that I am the Lord. They will be my people and I will be their God, for they will return to me with all their heart." (Jeremiah 24:7)

Spend some quiet time in the presence of God meditating on what it means to have a heart to know God. Write down any thoughts or insights.

WEDNESDAY
THOUGHTS FOR TODAY

There are several characteristics we must have if we are going to be eager learners of what God, as our Father, wants to teach. The first is the true *desire* to know Him and His will. God is not an exhibitionist. He will not reveal Himself to those who are less than passionate about knowing Him. The intense desire to learn of Him will express itself in a focused attention to God as our loving Father, a single-mindedness in learning about Him and from Him, and a growing drive to have an ever-deepening relationship with Him. This intensity of desire is the motivator. It is the driving force that causes us to commit the time and energy required to know God.

The second characteristic we need is a *commitment* to stay focused on Him. Knowing God does not happen all at once. It is an eternal process and requires a lifelong commitment. The sincere desire to be taught by God will result in our making it a priority to search the revelation we have been given in the Bible and to spend time in prayer so we learn to recognize His voice and to respond to His teaching.

The third characteristic we need to develop is *willingness to conform* to what He reveals. God sets standards and gives direction, much as a parent does with a child. We must conform to what He asks without question and in humble obedience. He will not teach Lesson #2 until we have learned and complied with Lesson #1.

THURSDAY
   THOUGHTS FOR TODAY

Yesterday we talked about desire, commitment and willingness to conform to what is revealed as characteristics needed if we truly desire to know God. The fourth characteristic is *acceptance* of the fact that there are things that we cannot understand fully while we are on earth and have the limited perspective of time and space. Our limitations do not mean that God is not willing to teach us; they only mean that we are limited in our ability to receive and perceive what He is teaching. There are eternal truths that we cannot even relate to on this side of heaven.

Jesus taught in parables in an attempt to bring spiritual concepts to a human understanding, and God describes heaven to us in language that we can relate to while we still live here on earth. The reality of what Jesus taught far exceeds the down-to-earth stories He told just as the beauty and magnificence of heaven far exceeds what we can imagine given our earthly limitations.

We should not be discouraged because we cannot understand *all* that God teaches us because there is a great deal that we *can* understand and learn. We also will find that, as we grow closer to Him and as our knowledge of God develops, we begin to understand more and more of what seemed mysterious to us as one time. As we grow in relationship to God, knowing Him becomes more important than knowing everything *about* Him and we joyfully accept the fact that mysteries exist, even as we anticipate their full revelation someday!

FRIDAY
   READING GOD'S MESSAGE

Proverbs 1:8; John 14:9; 1 Corinthians 14:26; John 16:13; Matthew 28:19-20

Look at each of these verses and write down what it shows you about how God teaches us about who He is:

Proverbs 1:8

John 14:9

1 Corinthians 14:26

John 16:13

What other ways can you think of God uses to teach us?

If you have learned about God in any of these ways, how can you use what you have learned to do what Jesus commanded in Matthew 28:19-20?

SATURDAY
FOR PERSONAL REFLECTION

Spend some time with God in prayer asking him these questions:

What priorities in my life need to change in order for me to learn more from You?

What are ways in which I need to be more in-tune with Your guidance in my life?

What other people should I be teaching about what I am learning from You?

Write down any thought that come to mind and then turn those thoughts into a prayer of commitment to knowing God.

SUNDAY

PRAYER

The Creator of the universe wants to spend time with me! That is what you are telling me, Lord, when You say, "Come to me, all you who labor and are heavy laden and I will give you rest". When you bid me to come and rest with You, that is an invitation of intimacy. It makes my heart dance with joy. What is the reason I wouldn't come running? I can't think of any at all. When You call me 'friend', let that wash over me like a refreshing drink of water to a thirsty soul. I will offer myself, my time and all I have to be one with You and the Father, Lord Jesus. I will never be done getting to know the depths of who You are and how much You are able to love me. Thank You for making me just the way I am. You love me and I can love me, too. Hallelujah! Amen!

WEEK SIXTEEN

Accessing Our Spiritual DNA

"The Christian does not think God will love us because we are good, but that God will make us good because He loves us." – C. S. Lewis

MONDAY
THOUGHTS FOR TODAY

We are God's adopted children and, as such, we are told that someday we will be like our older brother, Jesus. The things that happen to us in this life and the efforts we make to adapt our lives to the truth of Scripture are all working together to change us to look more like Jesus. We are members of God's family and it is the desire of His heart that we act like it. Getting there requires discipline. So we try. And we fail. We try harder. And we fail again. At some point in our Christian walk, we learn that our becoming like Christ is not of our own doing. God will grow us up into the image of Jesus if we simply allow Him to do so.

Richard Foster says it this way, "When we despair of gaining inner transformation through human powers of will and determination, we are open to a wonderful new realization: inner righteousness is a gift from God to be graciously received" (8). How do we receive that gift from God? First, we recognize that growth is a process. It does not happen magically and it does not happen instantly. Many of us give up as soon as we realize that the kind of development we want requires time, energy, and patience.

Sometimes we have to be content with first steps. If we are going to run a marathon, we need to exercise our muscles, eat the right foods, stay healthy, and get sufficient rest. Little by little, if we are disciplined in our approach, our bodies become fit and our running becomes easier and easier. Eventually, we are able to run the race and maybe even win it. We cannot win only by wanting to win. We need training. We will succeed in the endeavor only to the extent that we are disciplined athletes.

The same is true in our spiritual lives. We will not become spiritually mature overnight. Most likely, we will not suddenly lose our desire for the sin that is so tempting to us. We will not all at once find ourselves spending hours with God in prayer. We will not instantaneously understand the deep things of God which are hidden in His word. We will not wake up some morning being more loving, more patient, and more generous. All these areas require growth and that growth requires time and the discipline of placing ourselves in God's presence so He can change us.

TUESDAY
MEDITATION

". . . we are transfigured much like the Messiah, our lives gradually becoming brighter and more beautiful as God enters our lives and we become like him" (2 Corinthians 3:18 *The Message*)

Read this verse, then focus on a phrase or a few words that the Spirit directs you to. Meditate on those words, ponder them, allow them to take root in your soul. After a few minutes, write down any thoughts that come to your mind.

WEDNESDAY
THOUGHTS FOR TODAY

Perhaps the most important area of discipline for any human is the development of a God-centered *mind*. We cannot control thoughts that enter our minds, but we can control how long we let them stay there. Paul has a simple solution when he said, "we take captive every thought to make it obedient to Christ" (2 Corinthians 10:5b). Controlling our thought life will take discipline. But the more we do it, the easier it becomes. Thinking thoughts that are worthy of a child of the King will transform us. Allowing our minds to wallow in the mud of this earth and it skewed values will deform us. A disciplined thought life allows us to detach from this world and begin day-by-day to attach to the spiritual eternal world and to the heart of God and the mind of Christ.

A second important area of discipline relates to our *bodies*. We are told that our bodies are God's temples. The bodies we have are sacred places and God has entrusted us with their care. Caring for these bodies means that we must exercise physical and personal discipline in getting adequate sleep, choosing nutritional foods, engaging in appropriate exercise, obtaining medical care and counsel when needed, avoiding detrimental habits, and maintaining sexual purity. These kinds of habits are developed over time by the Holy Spirit in our lives as we surrender to His direction. He just awaits our cooperation as He does His transforming work in us.

THURSDAY
THOUGHTS FOR TODAY

For all of us there are times when we are not exercising the kind of personal disciplines that will bring us to spiritual maturity. Maybe we neglect the reading of God's Word or times of prayer, maybe we allow sin to creep into our lives, or maybe we begin to develop attitudes that are not in keeping with the image of Christ God desires for us. In these cases, God may choose to step in and lovingly correct us.

Since we know there are times when we may experience God's correction, one of the first questions we should ask when we are undergoing a time of hardship is whether or not God is sending the trouble as a discipline. God will never correct us without making sure we are aware of the reasons for the discipline any more than an earthly parent would punish a child without letting the child know what the offense was. So if we ask Him, He will reveal His purpose. If the hardship is for our correction, we will understand and we will have the opportunity to submit to the loving discipline of our Father. If the trial we face is not due to our sin, God will show us that, too, and we will know that God will walk with us through the difficulty and, by His grace, we will grow through it. Either way, we know that God has our best interest at heart and we will grow even in (and probably *especially* in) the tough times of our lives.

FRIDAY
READING GOD'S MESSAGE

2 Timothy 2:3-6

Read this passage that Paul wrote to Timothy as he was encouraging him in his spiritual growth. Then look at how each of the three examples teach us something about the ways by which we grow up spiritually. Write down what we can learn from each.

> Soldier:
>
> Athlete:
>
> Farmer:

SATURDAY
FOR PERSONAL REFLECTION

In what area of self-discipline are you the strongest? In what area are you the weakest? Are there any steps you can take now that will help you to train yourself in your weak areas?

How will focusing your thoughts on Jesus change the way you think? The way you dress? The way you talk to others? The way you worship? Think of ways you can focus more on Him today.

What should a member of God's family look and/or act like? Do you see yourself growing into that family resemblance more and more each day?

SUNDAY
PRAYER

Wonderful Counselor, You are helping me make the right choices as I grow up to be one with Jesus who is the head of the body. You keep assuring me that I am headed in the right direction and to be patient with myself as You are patient. I want more of the joy of seeing my real personality unfold as I let go of all the 'stuff' that has covered me up as I tried on other personalities that weren't of Your design. What a relief to start being a real and authentic human being instead of a human doing. Thanks for never giving up on me; and, Lord, help me not to give up on anybody either. With you all things are possible. Surprise me again, Jesus. I love you.

(8) Richard Foster, *Celebration of Discipline*, op. cit., pp. 6-7

WEEK SEVENTEEN

Asking for Help

"Often through the crises of our lives God communicates most powerfully to us." – Henry Blackaby

MONDAY

THOUGHTS FOR TODAY

Have you ever felt invisible? Have you ever felt that no one really saw you or knew you? Have you felt that no one really wants to hear what you think, that your opinions aren't important? Do your questions go unanswered? Are your expressed needs sometimes ignored?

Human beings let us down. Sometimes they are blinded by their own problems and sometimes they simply cannot see through the barriers we erect. There is always One to whom we are never invisible. God's eyes are always focused on us and His ear is always turned in our direction ready to listen with full attention when we talk to Him. His response is always one of love. We simply have to acknowledge our neediness and to express our desires to the One who knows us intimately.

Sometimes I think it hurts God that we are unwilling to ask Him to fill our most basic needs. As our loving Father, He is waiting with storehouses of provision for us, but wants us to express our reliance on Him and then allow Him to fulfill our desires. God's definition of spiritual maturity is greater and greater dependence on Him. Therefore, He continually encourages us to come to Him with both the mundane needs of our day and with the deepest needs of our hearts.

Specific examples are given throughout scripture of people who came to God when they had sinned, when they had doubts, when they had tried and failed, when they were criticized, when they were tired, when they had material or physical needs, and when they were afraid. God just invites us to come, to talk to Him, to tell Him what we need, and to know that He will answer our requests in the best possible way.

God's design is that we learn to depend on Him to meet all of the material, relational, emotional, and spiritual needs of our lives. This is a different mindset than we are accustomed to here on earth. We raise our children to become independent, to eventually move out of the house to earn a living, and to make their own way in the world. It's not like that in our relationship with God. He wants us to be continually more and more dependent on Him. In fact, He is raising us, not to *leave* home, but to *come* home. He wants us someday to sit around His great table in heaven as one great big family. God does not want to be an empty-nester!

TUESDAY

MEDITATION

"You do not have, because you do not ask God." (James 4:2b)

Ponder the truth of these words and allow the Holy Spirit to expand your vision of dependence on God for every need. Write down any thoughts that come to you.

WEDNESDAY

THOUGHTS FOR TODAY

The Old Testament prophet Daniel was famous for his consistent prayer life. The fact that he prayed three times a day at his window is what eventually got him into trouble with the king who wanted his subjects to bow to him alone.

We probably can learn something from the prayers of this godly man. In Daniel 9:18b-19a, he prays, "We do not make requests of you because we are righteous but because of your great mercy. O Lord, listen! O Lord, Forgive! O Lord, hear and act!" Here is what we might take away from Daniel's prayer:

1. We approach God, not because we are good enough but because He is merciful and promises to hear us. Our prayers are more about who God is than they are about who we are.
2. Then Daniel asks God to listen. It seems that God tends to hear and answer prayers that are prayed with honest passion.
3. Next, he prays for forgiveness. If we come to God in prayer

and are aware of sin in our life, we must confess it and receive His forgiveness and cleansing. Only then the way is clear for us to present our requests.
4. Those steps taken, Daniel's final request is for God to act. He spells out his specific needs and desires fully believing that the all-powerful, all-loving God will respond. We cannot get answers to prayers we do not pray!

THURSDAY
THOUGHTS FOR TODAY

We know that God, as our Father, will never respond to our prayers in a way that is less than 100% loving. We can go to Him knowing that we will find gifts from His hand that we do not deserve but that we truly need. So we approach Him sincerely, boldly, and confidently and then we thankfully accept His loving response. If we don't see an immediate answer to our requests, we should not assume that God has not heard us or that He will not answer.

Very often God's timing and ours do not coincide. We want answers right now. But God may be working many circumstances together to bring about the answer that will be best for us. We must allow Him the time to accomplish what He designs. That's where faith comes in: Believing God is answering even when what He is doing is not visible to us.

There are several ways in which God might answer our prayers. Sometimes we find the answer in the Bible. At other times, the Holy Spirit guides us. As children of God, we are given insight and counsel that are not available to the rest of the world. God will sometimes answer by changing circumstances in our lives. He will open particular doors of opportunity and close others. Then, we also know that God often uses other people to answer the requests we pray. And sometimes we are the "other people" who are the answers to prayer for someone else!

FRIDAY
READING GOD'S MESSAGE

Hebrews 11:6; 1 Chronicles 4:10; Psalm 13:1-2; Matthew 15:21-28

Read each of these passages and write down what you learn from each about the characteristics of effective prayer.

Hebrews 11:6

1 Chronicles 4:10

Psalm 13:1-2

Matthew 15:21-28

When God answers our prayers, we need to thank Him. But even when we feel that our prayers are not being answered, we should have a grateful spirit. Thank God for His loving care for you and for all that He has given you to enjoy.

SATURDAY

FOR PERSONAL REFLECTION

Why do you suppose God made it necessary for us to ask Him to meet our needs before He provides for them?

Do you sense a growing dependence upon God? If not, how can you learn to trust yourself less and Him more? If so, what do you think is helping you to grow in dependence?

Have you ever been the answer to prayer for someone else? Pray, asking God to provide opportunities for you to meet the needs of other members of your spiritual family.

SUNDAY

PRAYER

Holy Spirit, I am on my face before You asking You to show me what is my greatest necessity. Only You know what I need. I don't really know what is good for me. I thought I did at one time, but that was a lie. You are the Spirit of Truth and You are guiding me into all truth, a little at a time. Thank You for Your gentleness with me. I will stay here until I hear Your voice giving me distinct instructions. Where else can I go except to you? You alone have the words of eternal life and the unique path tailored just for me. Grant me grace as I wait on You. I am Your child and You are my Father. I pray in Jesus' holy name. Amen.

WEEK EIGHTEEN

The Family Resemblance

"God loves each of us as if there were only one of us." – St. Augustine

MONDAY

THOUGHTS FOR TODAY

You may remember the disclaimer that was going around a few years ago: *Please be patient. God isn't finished with me yet.* Aren't we glad He's not finished? That He has an end design in mind that will be far better that what we are now? That He hasn't given up on us? In fact, we have a pattern for what God's ultimate goal is for us. It is to become like Jesus. Once we are adopted into the family of God, Jesus becomes our elder brother, the One we look up to and emulate. The One we love and adore. If we are to become like Jesus, it seems that we can look at His life to get a pretty specific idea of the healthy spiritual and physical beings that God has in mind for us to be.

As we read in the Bible about Jesus' life and as we observe His works and listen to His teachings, we get glimpses into His behavior when He was here on earth:

- He was forgiving to those who acknowledged their weaknesses or sins.
- He was gentle with children.
- He was confrontational and sometimes angry with those who thought they knew it all and were, in their leadership, misleading others.
- He was compassionate toward the crowds who looked to him for spiritual teaching.
- He was merciful to the sick and infirm who came to Him for healing.
- His teaching had power and authority.
- He was in constant contact with His Father in heaven and was committed to fulfilling God's will in this world.

- He was never in a hurry or anxious or worried.
- He lived in this world but had an other-worldliness about Him that created a hunger for the spiritual in those who came to know Him best.

As we think about these characteristics, don't we sense a longing to be as whole, confident, productive, and peaceful as Jesus was? Don't we want to know the heavenly Father as He did and to join Him in accomplishing God's will in this world? Don't we desire to have our focus on the eternal instead of the temporary? How do we get there? How do we become like Christ? The answer is simple: Through developing a personal one-on-one intimacy with Him. Jesus invites us into an on-going, ever-deepening relationship with Him and the Father. When we accept that invitation, we find that the characteristics we see in Jesus will begin to appear in us, too. We start to look like Him!

TUESDAY
MEDITATION

"How great is the love the Father has lavished on us that we should be called children of God!" (1 John 3:1a)

Enjoy the wonder of the fact that you are God's child. Meditate on what it means to belong to Him, to experience His love, to have the security of knowing that you are in His family forever. Write down thought that come to your mind as you think about these things.

WEDNESDAY
THOUGHTS FOR TODAY

God is not stand-offish. He longs for intimacy with us, as dearly-loved members of His eternal family. We can have that closeness simply by having open hearts eager to learn all that we can about Him. If we are willing to learn, He is willing to reveal.

There are several ways we can learn more about God and His Son, Jesus. *First, we can dig into the Bible* to find out what is revealed about Him in the written text. The Bible is a great gift to us and is the most direct way for us to understand God, His expectations of us, and His dealings with mankind through history.

Second, we can look at God's creation and discover what He reveals about His personality in what He has created for us to enjoy! We can thank him for the beauty and bounty He has given and pray for wisdom in using it wisely and carefully.

Third, we can learn to recognize God's signature on people and events around us in the world. The Holy Spirit who lives within is will give us insight into these things. He wants us to know when God is at work in our lives or in the lives of those we love.

Fourth, we can talk to Him constantly. If we just ask, God will reveal His character, His personality, and His will to us so that we can know Him better, trust Him more, and serve Him with total commitment.

THURSDAY
THOUGHTS FOR TODAY

When we begin to experience God's love for us and realize that He is powerful enough to meet our needs and that He has a plan that is beyond our understanding, we begin to relax in our faith. We trust. And then our understanding of God begins to grow.

C. S. Lewis, in the *Chronicles of Narnia*, tells stories of Aslan, a great lion who is the representation of God to the earth children who come and go from the Land of Narnia where Aslan lives. Listen, as one time one of the children, Lucy, meets up with Aslan upon a return visit to Narnia.

"Welcome, child, "he said.

"Aslan," said Lucy, "You're bigger."

"That is because you are older, little one," answered he.

"Not because you are?"

"I am not. But every year you grow, you will find me bigger." (9)

As we grow in our faith, our view of God changes. One day, we look at God and realize that we see Him very differently than we did at one time. We realize that He is greater, bigger, and even more loving than we could have imagined earlier. He has not changed over the years, but we have. As we get closer to God, He reveals Himself to us and taking in more and more about Him changes us.

Eventually we become the "best possible version of ourselves, the version he originally created us to be – like Jesus." (10)

FRIDAY
READING GOD'S MESSAGE

Colossians 3:12-17

List the specific commands that Paul gives in this passage.

Write a description of what you think the family of God would look like if all Christians followed the directives in these verses.

Are there any of these commands that you need to be following more closely in your life? If so, write down specific things you feel God wants you to do in obedience to the teaching in this passage of scripture.

SATURDAY
FOR PERSONAL REFLECTION

Think about the life of Jesus, as you reflect on the following questions:

What do you admire most about the way He treated people?

How is He an example to you in His relationship with God the Father? What character traits of Jesus do you already see at work in your life?

What character traits of Jesus would you like to have more of in your life?

Write or say a prayer asking God to make you more like Jesus as you grow in your intimacy with Him. That is a prayer He will answer!

SUNDAY

PRAYER

Dear Lord, gracious Lord, kind Lord, I pray with your servant of old, Francis of Assisi, "Lord, make me an instrument of Thy peace. Where there is hatred. let me sow love. Where there is injury, pardon; where there is doubt, faith; where there is despair, hope; where there is darkness, light, where there is sadness, joy. O Divine Master, grant that I may not so much seek to be consoled, as to console; not so much to be understood as to understand; not so much to be loved as to love; for it is in giving that we receive; it is in pardoning that we are pardoned; it is in dying that we awaken to eternal life". Amen

(9)   C. S. Lewis, *Prince Caspian* (New York: HarperCollins, 1951, 1979).

(10)   Leslie Vernick, *How to Live Right When Your Life Goes Wrong* (Colorado Springs: Waterbrook Press, 2003), p. 193.

WEEK NINETEEN

When God Became Human

"The whole story of the world – and of how we fit into it – is most clearly understood through a careful, direct look at the story of Jesus." – Timothy Keller

MONDAY

THOUGHTS FOR TODAY

We have spent a few weeks now talking about our relationship to God as our Father in that He not only loves us, but also provides for us, protects us, listens to us, and teaches us. With that understanding as a foundation, we will now move on to getting our minds and hearts focused on Jesus – as the Word of God and as our eternal Redeemer. He did a great deal to make sure we could become His brothers and sisters. Ready to dig in?

Did you ever wonder what God is really like? We see evidence of His existence all around us and we sense His presence – at some times more than at others, but we have never shaken hands with Him, we have never looked Him in the eye, we have never had a conversation with Him like we might have with a friend over a cup of coffee. God is so different than we are in His very being that He knew we would have trouble understanding Him. Jesus became the solution to that problem; He became the 'bridge of knowing' between us and the creator God who is beyond human definition.

There is an old story about a man who looked outside one blizzard-ridden night and noticed that sparrows were suffering in the extreme weather and some were even dying. Sympathetic to their plight, he bundled up, braved the elements, and opened the big barn door so the birds could go inside to find shelter from the storm. They didn't move toward the barn, so the man began to shoo them in. This only frightened them and some flew away. The rest resettled in huddled bunches on their branches. The man then tried leaving a trail of birdseed they could follow into the barn. That didn't work either.

"If only I could communicate with them," he thought, "I could save their lives." But he could not talk "bird" and they, most certainly, didn't relate to the strange actions of this powerful and scary human. "If only I could become a bird even just for a few minutes," he thought, "then I could tell them in ways that they could understand how to get out of the cold and into the barn. If I were a bird, I could make them understand what I am trying to do for them."

Then, as he walked discouraged back into his cozy house, he realized that Jesus' coming to earth was God's means of communicating to us feeble humans the great plan of salvation that He had conceived and provided for us. Jesus left the warmth and safety of heaven, took on a human form, began to teach us about the Father God in heaven, and began to show us by His life the personality and character of our Creator. Jesus came to communicate God to us. The invisible God became visible. The God who is Spirit took on a human form. The unknowable became knowable. The untouchable could be touched.

TUESDAY
MEDITATION

"Anyone who has seen me has seen the Father. How can you say, 'Show us the Father'? Don't you believe that I am in the Father, and that the Father is in me? The words I say to you are not just my own. Rather it is the Father, living in me, who is doing his work." . . ." (John 14:9b-10)

Spend some time meditating on this verse and what it means for Jesus to be revealing God to men, women, and children on planet earth. Write down any thoughts that may come to you as you spend this time quietly in God's presence.

WEDNESDAY
THOUGHTS FOR TODAY

We would not have known the personality of God and His great love for us if Jesus had not come. We would not have understood God as our Father if Jesus had not introduced Him as such.

Instead, we would have seen only the God of the law and the Prophets in the Old Testament, a god who was set apart, holy, and difficult (even dangerous!) to approach. If Jesus had not spoken as human to human, we could not have understood that He was opening the doors to heaven for us, and that He invites us in out of the cold of the world and into the warmth and safety of relationship with him. Helping us grasp the true character of God is one of the primary reasons Jesus came to earth.

The second reason for his coming is to pay the price for our sinfulness. We are shocked and saddened at the physical suffering Jesus went through in His cruel treatment by men and His agonizing death on the cross. Seeing His suffering as a human being helps us to realize the extreme love He has for us. We recognize that it took great determination to face all these atrocities when He was actually the Son of God and could have called the whole thing off at any point. But He didn't. He completed the job He came to do including His triumphant resurrection from the grave.

Tomorrow we will look at the third (and seldom discussed) reason for Jesus coming to this planet.

THURSDAY
THOUGHTS FOR TODAY

The man in the story we read earlier would have become a bird, told them of the safety of the barn, been turned back into a man, and then would have gone back to the warmth of his living room. Jesus, too, returned to heaven after his three-decade (or so) sojourn on earth, but His story is different than that of the man and the birds. Jesus' taking on a human body meant that He would be changed forever. He did not return to heaven in the same condition in which He left it. Though His divine nature has never changed, as far as we can tell from Scripture, Jesus will always have a human body. It would be as if the man in our story, in his desire to save the birds, would always have to be a bird! There would be no returning to life as it once was.

Think of it! *Jesus never has separated Himself from human experience.* He is seated in a body at the right hand of God, fully human and fully God. What is He doing there? He stands in the gap between God and mankind. He communicates our need and His payment for our sins to God the Father. At the same time, He communicates God's holiness and love back to us. Only a person who is uniquely (but without sin) human and entirely God could qualify for this role. We have a Friend in high places who has not forgotten what it is like to be human, because He still shares the human condition with us.

FRIDAY
READING GOD'S MESSAGE

Hebrews 1:3; 2:14-18; 4:14-16

Hebrews 1:3: How does this verse support Jesus' purpose in revealing to us as humans the character of God?

What does this verse tell us about where Jesus is right now?

Hebrews 2:14-18: What reason is given in this passage for Jesus coming to earth?

Who does Jesus defeat?

From what fear does He release us?

Who was He sent to help?

What present role of Jesus is described in verse 17?

According to verse 18, why does Jesus having a body make Him a helper to us when we are tempted to sin? Hebrews

Hebrews 4:14-16: What is Jesus' role as our high priest?

Why are we able to approach Him confidently?

What will we receive?

SATURDAY
FOR PERSONAL REFLECTION

Spend some time thinking about the reasons for Jesus' coming to earth and write down your thoughts about how each affects you today:

His death and resurrection to redeem us:

His revealing to us what God is like:

His taking on a human body forever:

How does thinking about these things change the way you look at the significance of the sacrifices Jesus made for you?

What are you willing to give to Jesus out of sheer gratitude for His great gifts?

SUNDAY
PRAYER

Lord Jesus, when I lift up my hands to You, I am reminded of a little child that is asking to be picked up and carried. Lord, would you carry me today? I am tired of walking the walk today and I need You to pick me up. Thank You for giving me rest. Because You came in the flesh, I can imagine myself looking into Your eyes and seeing the love and acceptance You have for me. Let's just stay here awhile and look into each other's eyes. I need that. Thank You for being there for me 24/7. It is good to be here with You. Never let me go. I ask in Your name, representing all that you are. Amen.

WEEK TWENTY

God's Word in a Body

"The gospel is capable and designed to strike home in every culture, in every age, and in every language." – Scot McKnight

MONDAY

THOUGHTS FOR TODAY

At the funeral, Jessica told us that, during her last few hours of life, Margaret was quite quiet, sleeping on an off, drifting in and out of consciousness, and sometimes mumbling unintelligibly. Then, suddenly, she spoke in a clear voice, "Jesus," and she was gone. It was as if she saw Him, she recognized Him, and she simply went to Him. One word. One name. But the power carried with that reached all of us as we listened to the story. Later in the service, one woman spoke saying that she had sometimes doubted the existence of God and of heaven, but when she heard that Margaret had spoken Jesus' name as if in recognition, her faith was renewed. She said she now knew that God was real, heaven is an actual place, and Jesus is waiting to take us home.

What gives our words such power? The power to revitalize faith? The power to take away the terror of death? The power to soothe hurting hearts? The power to encourage and to provide hope? There is power in the words we speak because when we communicate in language, we are participating in the very nature of God. God is defined in scripture as "The Word". Since that is the case, why should we be surprised then, that when God speaks, things happen? Through words, the world was created, God's chosen people were established, and miracles occurred. His verbalization of himself is the essence of truth, enlightenment, activity, reality, and fullness. Word is the way in which He defines Himself to us and the way in which He has chosen to work in our world.

In early history, we find God communicating in words to men by appearing to them in human form or speaking from the clouds. At other times the Word came through prophets, visions, or angels. Then the Word began to be written as history, poetry, and prophecy. God revealed His message to humans who wrote down what they heard, saw and understood. The Bible began to take form and in it God began to open Himself up to us and to show us more about who He is.

Then the revelation of the Word became even clearer: When Jesus came, we were told in John 1 that "the Word became flesh." Jesus came to earth to embody the very essence of God which had been expressed only partially in past revelations. He is the perfect picture of the Creator God.

TUESDAY

MEDITATION

"For the Word of God is living and active . . . it judges the thoughts and attitudes of the heart." (portion of Hebrews 4:12)

Think about what this verse reveals about God as Word. Write down insights you are given about how you may need to look at God's revealed word with different eyes than you do today.

WEDNESDAY

THOUGHTS FOR TODAY

As we think about the ways God has chosen to use words to communicate to us, we see that He is stooping to our level to make sure we have as full an understanding of Him as possible. John Calvin referred to the Bible as "God's baby talk." God, because He is so far beyond our understanding, chose to use the simplest means of connection with us so we could get a glimpse of who He is and how much He desires a relationship with us. If God reached down so far as to use "baby talk" in the Bible, then becoming flesh was an even greater reach. God taking on a body had to feel as confining to God as putting on a straightjacket would feel to us. But Jesus was willing to take on human form so specific people at a specific time in history could see Him touch Him, observe His life, and ask Him questions. They could soak in all the understanding they could absorb during Jesus' years of public ministry and then, when He had left this earth, they would sit down with pen and ink at creaky wooden tables and try to reduce once again to words what Jesus had been like when He walked with them on earth's soil.

We were not there when Jesus walked this earth, but we have eyewitness records that we cherish and devour because of all they reveal to us about God through the Word made flesh who, for a time, lived on this earth.

THURSDAY
THOUGHTS FOR TODAY

It's not a surprise the words of Jesus had such power over people, over nature, over illness, over deformity, and over death itself when He was among us. What He desired, He spoke. What He spoke simply was. For example, we are given the account of the Roman centurion who came to Jesus because his son was dying. Jesus began to move toward the man's house, but the Roman protested that he was not worthy for Jesus to come under his roof. Instead, he said, "But just say the word and my servant will be healed." Jesus spoke and the servant immediately recovered. Jesus, just say the word and it is done. Just say what You want and it becomes reality in this world.

The Word no longer lives among us in a human body. He returned to God in heaven where He is today interceding for us. However, Jesus sent the third person of the Godhead, the Holy Spirit, Who lives within us. One of the roles of the Holy Spirit is to help us recall and understand what Jesus taught when He was on this planet. The Holy Spirit enlightens and empowers us through the living and powerful Word of God to live out the principles of God's kingdom in our world today. Through the power of the Word Who lived among us, His will continues to be accomplished in this world, but now *we* are the vehicles through whom it is done.

FRIDAY
READING GOD'S MESSAGE

1 John 1:1-4

Who wrote the book of 1 John? How did he know Jesus?

In verse 1, how does John use some of the five senses to tell about his personal knowledge of Jesus?

What two phrases does John use to describe Jesus in verse 1?

To what does John testify in verse 2?

What does John proclaim in verse 3?

What is the purpose of his telling about his knowledge of Jesus? (v.3)

Think of one way today that you can share with someone else what you have learned about God through your relationship with Jesus and His written word.

SATURDAY
FOR PERSONAL REFLECTION

Think about the words you say each day. As God's child, your desire is that your words honor Him and that they show to others the true character of God.

Write down the name of

someone you might encourage with your words.

someone you might gently correct with words of love.

someone to whom you might offer words of forgiveness.

someone who needs to hear words of hope.

Promise God that, if He gives you opportunity, you will use the words of your heart to make a difference in these lives. Then watch for Him to open doors!

What words do you need to hear today? Pray, asking God to speak

His words to your spirit. Write down whatever He brings to your mind.

SUNDAY
PRAYER

Father, help me to follow Your directions to be quick to listen, slow to speak and slow to get angry. Holy Spirit, let me hear Your voice telling me when and what to speak, give me Your power to listen to others' words with understanding and insight, and to give anger to you because I can't handle it; when I get angry, it only leads to trouble and broken relationships. You are giving me hope that through You, I can choose to tame my tongue. Holy Father, I want to be like Jesus, the made flesh. Speak Lord, your servant is listening. Amen.

WEEK TWENTY-ONE

Life-Changing Word

(About the Word of God): "We not only read and hear and inquire, but we meditate on what comes before us; that is, we withdraw into silence where we prayerfully and steadily focus upon it. In this way its meaning for us can emerge and form us as God works in the depths of our heart, mind, and soul." – Dallas Willard

MONDAY

THOUGHTS FOR TODAY

Jesus' words had power to bring about jaw-dropping miracles, that's not the only power they had. He used His words to teach as no had ever taught before. In fact, one of the purposes of His coming was to teach us what God is like and what He expects of us as mortals. Once Jesus got the attention of His followers by working miracles, He taught them, expressing giant God concepts in limited human language. Luke tells us that Jesus was found teaching in the temple every day. Even those who observed Him from a distance called Him "Rabbi". The rich young ruler addressed Him as "Teacher." The disciples asked Jesus to teach them to pray. Those who sat under the power of Jesus' words were amazed at His teaching. His teaching was out of this world! It astounded even the most educated of the time.

While we hear much about the life-altering miracles of Jesus' ministry, the words He used to teach have, by far, the greater long term benefit to mankind than the miracles He performed. The dead who were raised would die again. The paralytic who walked eventually lay still in the grave. The lepers who were cleansed are now silenced. But the words of Jesus' teaching live on and continue to reveal God to us.

Never before or since Jesus did God speak in physical form for a prolonged period of time to all who would listen. Never before or since Jesus did God subject Himself day-by-day to the expressed doubts and questions of His closest friends who were constantly probing to know more about who He was and what His plans were. God became this vulnerable, this touchable, and this knowable because He loves us and He *wants* us to know Him! The Word became flesh so humankind could interact with the living Word and be transformed by that interaction. I believe that the greatest miracles that Jesus performed were in the changed lives of those He left standing on the mount as He ascended back to heaven.

God's Word is just as life-changing today as it was when Jesus was here. To know that power, there are times when we must simply be wordless before the God who speaks. He desires to communicate with us. He waits patiently for us to become willing receivers of His messages of love and transformation.

TUESDAY

MEDITATION

"But the Lord is in his holy temple; Let all the earth be silent before him." (Habakkuk 2:18-20)

Focus on the words of these verses as you sit or bow in silence before God. Hearing God's voice is more a discipline than a gift. We wait expectantly and He speaks. Quiet your mind, quiet your body, quiet your inner voices, and listen in silence before our Lord. Write down any message He may give to you through thoughts that come to your mind.

WEDNESDAY

THOUGHTS FOR TODAY

When God speaks to us through His written message, the Bible, how should we respond?

First we should *believe what we read.* Believing that God has spoken is a reality that we will experience either now or at some time in the future. Remember this: God's desires will be fulfilled. His written Word reflects His desires. So, when God speaks, it is as if the spoken or written desire were already a reality. When Mary was pregnant with Jesus, she went to visit her cousin Elizabeth. When Elizabeth realized that her cousin was carrying the long-awaited Messiah, she responded in amazement and said, "Blessed is she who has believed that what the Lord has said to her will be accomplished." (Luke 1:45). In faith, we can claim the promises in the Bible. By faith, we can submit ourselves to the authority of God and be obedient to its requirements even if we don't understand the reasons why.

Second, we should *receive God's Word with prayer*. Prayer enables us to latch on to the power that is within the written of God. Through prayer we talk to our Father in heaven. Through prayer and words that flow through our thoughts, He reveals Himself and His reality to us. We talk, He talks. We speak and then we listen. Prayer aligns our will with God's will, our desires with His. The result is power in our prayers and power in the words by which we interact with God's written message.

THURSDAY

THOUGHTS FOR TODAY

As the power and authority of God's words become more real to us, we begin to realize the importance of the words we use when we talk to others and the thought words that we allow to remain in our own minds. If God is Word and His words have power to create or destroy, to build up or tear down, to energize or to diminish, our words, as His children, have similar (though lesser) characteristics. There are many people walking around today who are carrying wounds of words spoken to them as children, words spoken by people who may not have understood the power of their speech. There are others for whom the right word said at the right time and in the right way has set everything in order in their lives. Words wound and words heal.

Words also reveal. As we listen to others with open minds, we hear beyond their words and try to connect to the real needs of their hearts. Then we will be able to touch them effectively and creatively for the accomplishment of God's will in their lives and ours.

Lastly, recognizing the power of words, we will remember to surround ourselves with words that empower us to live as God intends. We can learn to recognize and dismiss negative messages based on lies and, instead, encourage ourselves with words of love and hope. We can fill our mind with Bible verses, good teaching, ennobling reading, and people who communicate gently and positively into our lives.

FRIDAY
READING GOD'S MESSAGE

John 1:1-18

In the first verse, what name does John give to Jesus?

How do we know that John considers Jesus, as the Word, to be God?

According to verses 3 and 10, Who created the world?

How does creation illustrate for us the power of the spoken word?

According to verse 14, who does Jesus reveal to us?

In verse 17, what kind of message did Jesus come to reveal?

What does receiving Jesus' message enable us to do (v. 12)?

SATURDAY
FOR PERSONAL REFLECTION

Think about a time when the words someone said to you had a powerful effect on the way you viewed yourself. Maybe the speaker of those words was a teacher, a parent, a grandparent, or a trusted friend.

Why do you think words have such power over us?

Who are the people around you who look to you for affirmation and approval?

Think of ways in which you can identify their strengths or their potential. Then intentionally begin to use your words to empower them to be what God created them to be.

Then bring those persons to prayer and, by your words to God, you will open the power of heaven to work in the lives of those you touch with your words here on earth.

SUNDAY
PRAYER

Lord, through Your loving words to me and Your drawing me to You. You are showing me that loving You is the highest form of worship. You want me and You to be in this loving relationship. Now I know what You mean it when You say that You are a jealous God. Thank You for being jealous of any other lovers that I might choose to take over You. I don't want to break your heart by being unfaithful. Thank you, Holy Spirit, for brooding over me and keeping me close to You. You are soul of my soul. Loving You is good for me and for those around me. Let the love flow. We ask in Jesus' name. Amen.

WEEK TWENTY-TWO

The Power of the Word

"Words create. God's word creates; our words can participate in creation." – Eugene Peterson

MONDAY

THOUGHTS FOR TODAY

You may have heard the story of the college student who set out for class one day in fine form. Little did he know that his friends were using him as a psychological experiment. They had pre-arranged to casually meet up with him at various times on his way to and from his first two classes of the morning. The first commented that he looked a little pale. The second asked if he felt all right. The third expressed concern for his health. By then, the student, who had felt healthy and strong that morning, packed up his books and headed back to the dorm because he was feeling really sick!

The power of words moves us, creates feelings in us, and even changes our physical well-being. If we know that to be true, then we should guard carefully the words that we take into our inner selves. When we think of the bombardment we are subject to each day with television, radio, e-mail, texts, tweets, telephones, and reading materials, we realize that many of the words we are exposed to are not uplifting and may, in fact, cause us discouragement or anxiety and some may lead us away from God. I have found that I am more able to stay focused on my eternal values if I protect myself (the "off" button is a great spiritual tool!) against words that should not be part of my life.

This is an important point to remember, as well, in the self-talk in which we engage moment by moment. We need to care for our souls by speaking words of nourishment and encouragement and truth, not by engaging with self-deprecating commentary on who we are or what we have done. God's Word tells us we are His dearly loved children and we need to agree with God on that point and verbally confirm ourselves within ourselves. We should never be less kind to ourselves than God is to us!

God's words are those of love, mercy, grace, and peace, but

also of holiness, separation, and commitment. These are the kinds of words we should be focused on, they are the words we should put into practice in our thoughts and in our conversations. And, then, once we have connected with the living Word, we have the responsibility we have of carrying the His message into the world around us.

TUESDAY

MEDITATION

". . . man does not live on bread alone but on every word that comes from the mouth of the Lord." (Deuteronomy 8:3b)

Think about the words of this verse and ask God to teach you from it. Write down anything that comes to your mind as you mediate in His presence.

WEDNESDAY

THOUGHTS FOR TODAY

As followers of God, our words are full of power to change people not just in terms of how they feel today, but also in how they may be affected for eternity. As Jesus said to His disciples, "The words I say to you are not just my own. Rather, it is the Father, living in me, who is doing his work." (John 14:10). Then He goes on to promise that when he leaves the earth, the Holy Spirit will come to live in them (this promise is, of course, for us, too) and "On that day, you will realize that I am in my Father, and you are in me, and I am in you." (v.20). We have the very person of God, the living Word residing within us. As we yield to that Spirit-in-residence, our words take on power that we never knew they could have.

Let's think about that. If God is the Word and, as such, the Word is the expression of who God is and what He desires, then when our words line up with His Word, there is power. When our desires are the same as the desires of God, they will be fulfilled. That is why Jesus went on to say in the same conversation with His disciples, "You may ask for anything in my name, and I will do it." (John 14:4). When God speaks, things happen. When our words are consistent with the Word, we can expect interesting things to happen.

THURSDAY
THOUGHTS FOR TODAY

How do we use words today in a way that is consistent with the living, powerful Word of God? Presenting the message of the gospel is one way. Conversations that we have with other people is another. There are those who say that just the simple, silent living of our lives will direct people to God.

That may be so, but it is apparent that God has ordained words to have the power to bring people to a point of understanding and decision: Preaching, teaching, sharing, reading, and writing. These are all ways of using words to communicate the message of God to this world. We do the best we can with this task, but should always remember that ". . . no man can adequately teach and explain a single Word of God with all his words. It is an eternal Word and must be understood and contemplated with a quiet mind" (11). From that place of quietness we simply share what we have learned through God's message to us.

Once we have experienced the living Word of God, we would rather die than lose our communicative connection with Him. God's words not only open the door to relationship with Him, they become the *essence* of that relationship. When we are eternally in His presence, we may no longer need words in order to fully relate to Him. But for now, words are our lifeline to the living, creative God – and Jesus came to make sure we knew that!

FRIDAY
READING GOD'S MESSAGE

Psalm 119:9-16

Every verse in this psalm refers to God's in some way (commandments, precepts, law, etc.). Read all the verses in this section and write down the word or words in each verse that refer to the Word of God.

What two requests to this writer make of God (vv. 10 and12)?

What does he do to strengthen his relationship with God (vv. 9-11, 13-6)?

In what ways does his commitment to God's help him to live a better life (vv. 9, 11)?

What promise does he make in verse 16?

SATURDAY
FOR PERSONAL REFLECTION

Make a list of all the ways you take in words each day. Are there any of those sources that you should eliminate or cut back on? Are there any which you should devote more time to?

Think about the self-talk you engage in each day. Are the messages you give yourself positive or negative? Ask God to help you recognize the lies you sometimes tell yourself and write down any that come to your mind. Next time that message comes, recognize it as a lie and dismiss it from your thoughts.

Think about the words you speak each day. Are they uplifting and encouraging to others? Do you need to cleanse your language? Do you need to weigh your words before your speak them? Write down any thoughts that come to your mind about guarding your speech so that the power of your words will lift up and not tear down.

SUNDAY
PRAYER

Father, Your voice is the most beautiful voice; You always speak in love, always with my best interest in mind, and give directions that are helpful. Sometimes You speak very firmly and sometimes You may seem pushy, but You always speak in love. When I hear a voice that is accusing or condemning, I know that is not You, my loving Father, but an unclean spirit vying for my attention. Harshness is not a part of Your voice either. Spending time with You and Your Word, the Bible, has helped me to know Your voice. Thank you for continuing to draw me to Your side. There's no place like being at home with You, Father. Thank You, Jesus, for taking me to the Father, and thank You, Holy Spirit, for showing me Jesus. I love you. Amen.

(11) Brennan Manning, *Ragamuffin Gospel* (Colorado Springs: Multnomah Books), p.45.

WEEK TWENTY-THREE

The Ultimate Sacrifice

"Let every man sanctify the Lord God in his heart and he can thereafter do no common act. For such a man, living itself will be sacramental and the whole world a sanctuary." – A. W. Tozer

MONDAY
THOUGHTS FOR TODAY

Do you remember the account of Moses going to Pharaoh (at God's insistence) to demand that Pharaoh release the Israelites from their slavery? Of course, Pharaoh was not very enthused about losing the valuable workforce he had inherited, so he said "no". Saying "no" to God is never a good idea and Pharaoh found that out through a series of ten plagues which completely devastated the land of Egypt. The last plague was the final straw, though, and that particular plague has become a focal point of all of history.

God forewarned the Israelites that, as His final punishing plague against Egypt, He was going to kill the firstborn male in every household on a particular night. However, there was a particular protection offered for those who honored the one true God. Every family who believed God was to choose a year-old male lamb without defect. On the appointed day, they were to slaughter the animal and use its blood to mark the doorposts of their homes thereby signaling to the angel of death that this was a God-honoring home. Upon seeing the blood, the angel of death would pass over the house and move on to strike only in the homes of those who had not obeyed God's instruction. The angel came, every unmarked household (mostly Egyptians) suffered a tragic death, and the Israelites who had obeyed God's instructions were spared from death and freed by Pharaoh.

The remembrance for salvation that God gave to the people that day became an annual celebration in the land of Israel that endures to the present time. It is called Passover and provides a vivid picture of a lamb taking the place of the otherwise-doomed firstborn son. Over time the Israelites came to understand that the Passover was a picture not only of the rescue from Egypt and the saving of the

Israelite sons, but also was a foretelling of the means by which God would offer redeem the entire world through the coming of His Son as a human being.

We have seen these past weeks that the purposes in Jesus taking on a human body included the revelation of God to us by the way He lived and, as the living Word, by what He taught. But there is more to the story. This week we will focus on the sacrifice Jesus came to make and how it satisfied God's demands for both justice and mercy.

TUESDAY

MEDITATION

"I have been crucified with Christ. My ego is no longer central. It is no longer important that I appear righteous before you or have your good opinion, and I am no longer driven to impress God. Christ lives in me. The life you see me living is not 'mine', but it is lived by faith in the Son of God, who loved me and gave himself for me." (Galatians 2:20 *The Message*)

Read the verse slowly and meditatively two or three times. Then choose a phrase that seems of particular importance to you and spend a few minutes meditating on those words. Write down anything that comes to your mind after your time of meditation.

WEDNESDAY

THOUGHTS FOR TODAY

One Passover eve nearly 2,000 years ago in Jerusalem, Jesus sat at the table celebrating the ceremonial feast with His disciples. The meal they shared consisted of several items, but the most important to the ceremony were the wine, the unleavened bread, the bitter herbs, and the lamb. The readings and prayers associated with each cup of wine and each portion of the meal served as remembrance of the past, praise to God for His deliverance, and a looking forward to the Messiah who was to come as the perfect Lamb of God.

After that meal, Jesus was arrested and then suffered all night until the following morning when He was sentenced to die. While preparations for His crucifixion were happening outside the city walls that Passover day, the high priest back at the temple in Jerusalem was making preparations, too. The lamb was made ready because at exactly 3:00, as was the custom, the innocent animal's throat would be slit, its blood drained out, and its life taken in remembrance of the Passover that had occurred in Egypt 1,500 years earlier.

Meanwhile that morning, Jesus was nailed to the cross where He would hang until death. We know that Jesus suffered indescribably during this time and that He willingly gave up His life as had been foretold at Passover long ago. But, at last, Jesus spoke His final words and died. It was 3:00, exactly at the moment when the priest was slaughtering the Passover lamb. God's details are precise!

THURSDAY
THOUGHTS FOR TODAY

Jesus' sacrifice for us is superior to the old sacrificial system in several ways. *First, the writer of Hebrews tells us that Jesus' death not only paid the penalty for our sins, but also cleanses our consciences.* Jesus takes away our guilt. This is good news for a world in which psychologists tell us that much of the depression rampant in our society relates to unresolved guilt!

Second, we are also told in Hebrews that Jesus' sacrifice was a one-time event. It is no longer necessary for us to offer animals in payment for our sins. All the sins we have ever committed and all that we will still commit before we die are paid for by Jesus' death.

Third, Jesus' sacrifice actually gives us the power to live purer, nobler, more sanctified lives. This is something the sacrificial lamb of the Old Testament was certainly not able to do. Once we accept Christ's ultimate gift, we do not walk away unchanged. We are given new natures, natures that now can choose to follow God, can overcome sin in our lives, and can do good in this world. Paul tells us in Galatians that if we could achieve the kind of rightness that God requires by following a list of rules, Jesus would not have had to die. But just trying harder has never made us better. We can become whole only by receiving the gift of grace and mercy that

Jesus has provided. Then, we can give up trying and begin trusting as we follow Him!

FRIDAY
READING GOD'S MESSAGE

Hebrews 10:1-25

If, as verses 3 and 4 state, it was impossible for the blood of bulls and goats to take away sin, why did God ask the people to offer these sacrifices?

The writer tells us in verses 10 and 14 that those of us who are followers of Christ are made perfect and are being made holy. What do you think the writer is trying to help us understand?

Jesus' sacrifice for us allows us to come to God in a new way. According to verse 22, how can we now approach God?

What purposes for meeting with other Christians are given in verses 24 and 25?

SATURDAY
FOR PERSONAL REFLECTION

What is one thing you can do today to show Jesus how grateful you are that He became the once-and-for-all sacrifice for your sins?

What is one thing you can pray boldly about today because you know that Jesus opened the way for you to approach God with confidence?

What is one sin that you need to bring before God in confession so He can continue to make you holy?

Who is one person you can encourage in his or her walk with God today?

SUNDAY

PRAYER

Thank you, Jesus, for holding out Your arms to me and, with the love in Your eyes, inviting me to run into Your arms. You are always ready to receive me as I run to You. Just hold me; Your presence is all I need to quiet me and calm my fears and anxieties. You make the way smooth; You have brought every mountain low and raised up every valley. You did this through the cross; You suffered and died and rose again for me. Every day is a new start; You never tire of picking me up, dusting me off and getting me back on the path of life. You are the path of life. Lead on, O King eternal. Amen.

WEEK TWENTY-FOUR

Touching the Eternal

"We need never shout across the spaces to an absent God. He is nearer than our own soul, closer than our most secret thoughts" –
A. W. Tozer

MONDAY

THOUGHTS FOR TODAY

There is the story of two men camping in a wilderness area who were awakened in the night by a howling windstorm. As the storm subsided, they lay quietly in their sleeping bags gazing up at the night sky from which the clouds were now clearing. One of them began to think lofty thoughts about creation and the immensity of the world around him. As he gazed heavenward, he commented on the beauty of the sky, the millions of the brilliant stars, and the relative insignificance of man. Then he turned to his companion and says, "And what do *you* see?"

The second man, who was rooted in the practicalities of life, said, "What I see is that our tent has blown away." It's all a matter of perspective, isn't it? One of the great gifts that Jesus gave to us by His life on earth was a brand-new perspective on the life we are living. He has helped us to see beyond the missing tent into the realm of mystery, beauty, and eternity.

Robert Frost once said, "In three words I can sum up everything I've learned about life: "It goes on." Life does go on. It goes on day-by-day now, but because of Jesus' revelation to humanity, we know that it will go on without end after we leave this earthly existence. What was so unusual about Jesus' life and teaching that forever changed the way we look at eternity?

When Jesus came to this earth, He was moving from eternity into time, from a place of forever to a place of beginnings and endings. Jesus was the second person of the triune God before He took on a human body, He remained God during his time with humanity, and He continues to be God now that He has returned to heaven. While there was no interruption of His eternal nature, there was an interruption of the condition and position in which He existed.

But because He was an eternal being who had taken on human form, He could communicate concepts of eternity to us mere mortals. He brought the light of eternity to everything He did, every relationship He cultivated, every person He encountered, and every plan that He unfolded. We got glimpses of a life beyond this world. By observing Jesus and listening to what He taught, humankind began to see the immense sky beyond the tent.

TUESDAY
MEDITATION

"Now this is eternal life: that they may know you, the only true God, and Jesus Christ, whom you have sent."" (John 17:3)

Meditate on this verse which defines eternal life for us. Write down any thoughts that come to your mind as you ponder this truth.

WEDNESDAY
THOUGHTS FOR TODAY

Do you ever feel that time is your enemy? That time either flies by too fast when your to-do list is overwhelming or moves at a snail's pace while you wait for the pain to pass? For God it's different. He lives outside of time. When there is no time, there is no past, present, and future. Every moment is now. There is no time running out, or flying by, or dragging on with God.

In fact, Jesus' first miracle was an expression of His eternal nature as a being who lived outside the confines of time. He attended a wedding in a small town in Galilee and was asked if He could help because the hosts were running out of wine. Jesus instructed the servants to fill with water the stone vessels used for ritual washing. They obeyed, filling the 20-plus gallon jugs to capacity. When the servers began to pour out the water, they discovered that it was not water, but wine! Now, what is the difference between fruit juice and wine? A few key ingredients and the passing of time to allow fermentation to occur.

This miracle shows us Jesus' power over time. Compressing months into minutes was as easy for Him as asking for the water to be poured out. Isn't it encouraging to know that if we make Jesus the master of our time, we can be sure that we have enough of it to accomplish in any given day when He wants us to do?

THURSDAY
THOUGHTS FOR TODAY

Eternity does not begin when we die but, rather, it encompasses time itself. Jesus showed us that we are living eternity right now, but because we are in the time portion of eternity, we are limited in the scope of our understanding. Therefore, we often do not realize the eternal value or lack of value of the activities in our lives. It may be that one conversation, one encounter, one decision, or one touch will have an everlasting effect that we cannot yet see. It may be that the things to which we dedicate great amounts of time have no value beyond this world.

His understanding of eternity is what caused Jesus to turn the values of this temporary world upside down. His famous Sermon on the Mount pointed out that simply obeying the law was not enough. God, Jesus told us, was looking for changed hearts and transformed lives. He said it was not enough to resist the temptation to kill our neighbor when he angered us. God's expectation was that we would love our neighbor in spite of his unlovability. He said that the last would be first and the first last. He taught that the greatest in His kingdom was the one who served. Jesus saw beyond this life into eternity and tried to convey to those who were willing to listen that the significance of what we do here and who we become here will not be revealed until we are beyond the confines of time and the world that we now know.

FRIDAY
READING GOD'S MESSAGE

John 3:1-18

Read this story of Jesus' discussion with Nicodemus as he tries to help a human being understand some eternal concepts. Then think about the following questions:

How does Jesus' concept of new birth help us understand the difference between earthly life and eternal life?

How does the illustration of the invisible wind give a picture of the eternal spiritual world?

What did Jesus give as His credentials for teaching these things?

What does verse 16 reveal to us about God's plan?

SATURDAY
FOR PERSONAL REFLECTION

Think about what you have to accomplish in the next few weeks. What practices can you adopt that will allow God to have control over your schedule?

Here are some methods you might consider:

- Praying over every appointment *before* you accept it.
- Committing each day, as it begins, to God and inviting Him to add to or delete from your plans so you know you will do what He wants you to do that day.
- Watching for opportunities each day to give a glimpse of God's eternal values to those whose lives you touch.

Pause now to acknowledge the eternal God as the one to whom you are responsible for your use of time and thank Him that, if you trust Him, He will enable you to accomplish all that He wants you to do.

SUNDAY
PRAYER

Lord, help me to follow the direction in your Word that says, "Today, please listen, don't turn a deaf ear as in the bitter uprising." (Hebrews 3:8 The Message). I have only today, and if I obey You today, then tomorrow will take care of itself. Now is the time! Lord, I confess that I procrastinate and put You off. Today I will choose to turn my procrastination over to You, put it in Your nail-scarred hands and receive back Your grace to listen well and to cheerfully obey today. You have made me glad! Amen.

WEEK TWENTY-FIVE

Living in Eternity's Light

"Christ liberates me from my bondage to the individual moments that compose the brief years of my life. In Him, I live forever. I surpass time." – Calvin Miller

MONDAY
THOUGHTS FOR TODAY

Russian author Leo Tolstoy tells a story about a king who was trying to find the answers to three important questions:

How can I know the right time to do everything?
Who are the most necessary people in my life?
How can I know what is the most important thing to do at any given time?

He felt that if he knew the answers to these questions, he would go down in history as a great leader of his people. So, the king disguised himself as a commoner and went into the woods to seek the advice of a hermit who was reported to be a wise man. The hermit was digging silently in his garden and did not answer the king when he asked his questions. As he watched, the king began to feel sorry for the bowed down old man so he took a hoe and dug beside him.

He was about to leave, disappointed that he did not receive answers to his questions, when a man, bleeding profusely, came staggering out of the woods. The king and the hermit tended the man's wounds, and after a watchful night, knew they had saved his life. In the morning, the injured man explained that he had been an enemy of the king and had followed him from the castle to the hermit's hut. The man decided to wait until the king began his return home so he could attack and kill him along the way. Instead, while he waited in the woods and the king showed kindness to the hermit by working in the garden, the would-be-attacker was assaulted by others and severely injured. He stumbled to the hermit's cottage for help. Now he humbly thanked the king for his great kindness and swore new allegiance to the kingdom.

At that point, the hermit was able to answer the king's three questions this way: "Remember then: there is only one time that is important – now! It is the most important time because it is the only time when we have any power. The most necessary man is he with whom you are, for no man knows whether he will ever have dealing with anyone else; and the most important affair is to do him good, because for that purpose alone was man sent into this life!" (12)

TUESDAY

MEDITATION

"Teach us to number our days aright, that we may gain a heart of wisdom" (Psalm 90:12)

Meditate on this prayer and make it yours. Write down any thoughts that come to mind as you wait in God's presence.

WEDNESDAY

THOUGHTS FOR TODAY

We never know when we touch eternity. We go about our lives and do what we do aware only of the choices we make about how to use the time we have in any given day. But, once in a while, a word we say or an action we take has a consequence far beyond that which we can see at the time. Tolstoy's king had no idea of the significance of the choices he made that day, but being where he was when he was and helping when he could may have saved his life and, in the larger view of things, may have saved his country from civil war.

With the wisdom of the tale in mind, let us commit to fully experiencing the brief earthly lives we have been given. We put aside the past, we trust God for the future, and we dig into the moment that we are living right now. Life becomes more real, more alive, more vibrant, and more meaningful because of the eternity of which it is a part. Not one minute of this life that we experience is insignificant. All of our minutes reach into eternity where God Himself infuses them with value and power.

The psalm writer reminds us that, "Each man's life is but a breath." (Psalm 39:5b). When we realize temporary nature of our lives, we place more value each day and we live fully moment-by-moment as we pass through time.

THURSDAY
THOUGHTS FOR TODAY

Because of our human limitations, we are driven to dependence on Jesus to guide us so that our day-by-day decisions will have eternal significance. He is the eternal one who knows the ends of our life stories, who sees into every moment of our lives and gleans from each their essential value.

We grasp eternity by giving up on figuring out our place in the world and in the eyes of those around us and, instead, beginning to trust in the unseen significance in the daily events of our lives, allowing Jesus to bring eternity to them. We will begin to understand that we live for a world beyond time, a world of far greater reality than this one, a world we do not yet see, but believe exists because Jesus told us about it. Once we grasp even a bit of that truth, our living in this world of time is forever changed.

The Jesus of eternity knows far more than we do about what decisions we should be making today. He knows the outcome of our plans. He knows the significance of our relationships. In prayer, we give up control to Him, trading our worry for trust and our anxieties for peace. With our future securely in His hands, we are ready to enter into the adventure of the moment. We do that by practicing attentiveness to people around us, to our own feelings, to our senses, and to our connection to God.

FRIDAY
READING GOD'S MESSAGE

Luke 12:15-34

In these verses, Jesus teaches His followers to have an eternal perspective as they make daily decisions. Think about these questions:

What was the daily focus of the rich man?

Why was that a foolish choice?

What command does Jesus give in verse 22? Is that an easy command for you to obey?

What do you think Jesus means by saying, in verse 31, to seek God's kingdom?

What do you see as the truth of Jesus' concluding statement in verse 34?

SATURDAY
FOR PERSONAL REFLECTION

When your mind is relaxed, what kinds of thoughts does it naturally go to?

Are these thoughts consistent with Jesus' teaching in the Luke passage we studied yesterday?

If not, what are some steps you can take to make sure that your priorities are consistent with those that Jesus taught?

On what eternal values should we be focused?

Is there anything in your life taking time and attention that should be eliminated so your day-to-day can be more consistently aligned with eternal values?

SUNDAY
PRAYER

Lord, I want my mind renewed. I'm tired of being selfish, of being fearful and lacking courage to step out in faith when You speak. Increase my ability to act on the faith that You have given me and not focus on what I lack. There is so much pain and hurt in the world; can one person make a difference? You remind me that You were one person and you changed the world. Now You are offering me Your life to go and do the same. You have such trust in me. Can it be that the Creator of the universe trusts me to carry on His work of love? A walk of love in an eternal purpose every day is possible. I will begin in your name, Jesus. Amen.

(12) Leo Tolstoy, *Walk in the Light* (Maryknoll, New York: Orbin Books), pp. 347-351.

WEEK TWENTY-SIX

Designed for Relationship

"Love is the only force capable of transforming an enemy into a friend." - Martin Luther King, Jr.

MONDAY

THOUGHTS FOR TODAY

We have learned a lot about knowing God in our study together and have dug into such topics as salvation, the Word of God, and eternity. Now, let's see if we can see how all of that makes a difference our relationships with other people. Most of us have a lot to learn in that area, so let's begin.

If we did man-on-the-street interviews and asked people the goal of their lives, what do you think they would say? Many answers would involve the word "happiness." You and I want to be happy and so does every other human being on the face of this planet. God wants us to be happy, too, but sometimes He goes about bringing us to the point of true happiness in a seemingly round-about way. Or maybe He just knows us well enough to know that, in order to be truly happy, we have to learn the fine art of self-sacrifice.

The very first chapters of the Bible give the account of God's creation of this earth and everything in it. There were six days of creation and at the end of each one, God pronounced His creation as "good". Except the sixth day. On that day He had created Adam and, as He looked at this man-creature, made in the image of God himself, God did not say "It is good." Instead, He said, "It is *not* good for man to be alone." So, He continued His creation by the forming a woman, taken from man's side, to be a companion and helper for him.

It was not good for Adam to be alone. It's not good for us to be alone, either. God designed us humans to need one another. In that need, we are driven to find each other, to enjoy companionship, and to be able to give and receive help as we navigate the waters of life. Sounds idyllic, doesn't it? Why is it, then, that the closer we get to someone, the harder it is to see the ideal? We need each other desperately, but sometimes being close to someone is like hugging a porcupine – more pain than pleasure. Maybe God should have thought through this plan of companionship a little more carefully! Or maybe He did.

God knew that, in order for us to become all that He wants us to be, in order for us to have the rough edges smoothed off so we can be a beautiful sculpture in God's very image, in order for us to grow up as spiritual beings, we had to learn to adapt, to love, to give, to sacrifice, and to serve. Nothing will teach us those life lessons more effectively than entering into a long-term committed relationship with another human being whether it is as an employee, church member, child, spouse, parent, or friend.

TUESDAY

MEDITATION

". . . if we love one another, God lives in us and his love is made complete in us." (I John 4:12b)

Meditate on the words of this verse and ask God to show you how His love can be made complete in you. Jot down your thoughts as you sit in His presence.

WEDNESDAY

THOUGHTS FOR TODAY

Remember how Jesus summed up all the commandments that people of His day were trying to live up to? He said, "Love the Lord your God with all your heart and with all your soul and with all your mind. . . and love your neighbor as yourself. All the Law and the Prophets hang on these two commandments" (Matthew 22:37-40). The people of Jesus day got caught up in the details, in the fine points of right and wrong, and they missed the big picture which Jesus summarized in two simple commands to love.

Think about it. If we learn to love in the spiritually mature way that God wants us to grow into, we will treat those around us as we would treat Jesus Himself if He appeared bodily in front of us. We would be willing to serve, willing to lose an argument now and then, willing to give up what we want for the sake of the person we love.

Even though we cannot love perfectly, if we allow our hearts to get softer toward the people with whom we relate closely, that very softness will open doors to love. We would not keep track of the wrongs of the past, but would look toward reconciliation of differences and forgiveness for earlier offenses. We would begin to see other people through Jesus' eyes of love. We get to choose how we will respond to other people in our lives. What choice are we making today?

THURSDAY
THOUGHTS FOR TODAY

When Jesus gave the command to his 1st century hearers to love God with all their hearts and to love their neighbors as themselves, one listener asked Jesus to explain who his neighbor was. Why do you suppose he asked that question? I think he was trying so hard to follow the letter of the law and that he didn't want to miss doing anything he was supposed to do. He wanted to do everything right so he could not be criticized. He wanted to make sure he "loved" everybody he was commanded to love.

Jesus answered him by telling the parable of the Good Samaritan and, indicating by that story, that our neighbor is anyone who needs us to be in relationship with him or her. There is no letter of the law in the Samaritan's service to the injured man. There is only the law of love.

If we choose to follow Jesus' law of love, we will find, over time, that we begin to think less often of ourselves and our own needs and more and more about meeting the needs of others. We will delight in finding ways to serve and to give, even at great cost to ourselves. And then, when we least expect it, we may realize that we are becoming more and more like Jesus, not by exerting the effort to do so, but by making relationship choices that are based on love and not on obligation.

FRIDAY
READING GOD'S WORD
Luke 10:25-37

As you read this familiar parable, think about the following questions:

What was the questioner's motivation in asking his question?

What is the significance of the priest and the Levite passing by the wounded man in the story?

How did the Samaritan feel when he saw the wounded man? What does that tell you about his motive in helping him?

What do you think Jesus was communicating when He said, "Go and do likewise"?

SATURDAY
FOR PERSONAL REFLECTION

Think about the long-term, committed relationships in your life.

Which of them are healthy and fulfilling?

To what do you attribute the good quality of these relationships?

Which of them are troubling and difficult?

What can you do to soften your heart toward difficult people and open the doors to a love-based relationship?

Pray, asking God to allow you to see people in your life as Jesus would see them if He were in your place. Write down any insights you gain.

SUNDAY
PRAYER

Holy Spirit, thank You for revealing to me that I need more of Your fruit of love. I do ask for more love. Please start now to show me how to be kind and loving. I need Your definition of kindness. I am aware that kindness draws people together and that is what You want from Your children----staying close to each other. Prepare me for this; Help me to get rid of wanting to be independent and isolated. I need you and I need others and I need to show them Your love. I will await Your transforming power in me. Surprise me; Your timing is exciting to watch. I adore you, Father, Son and Holy Spirit. You are my only reality. I want to know You better. I ask for this in Jesus' powerful name. Amen.

WEEK TWENTY-SEVEN

The Importance of Honesty

"Above all, don't lie to yourself. The man who lies to himself and listens to his own lie comes to a point that he cannot distinguish the truth within him, or around him, and so loses all respect for himself and for others. And having no respect, he ceases to love." - Fyodor Dostoyevsky

MONDAY
THOUGHTS FOR TODAY

"Do you swear to tell the truth, the whole truth, and nothing but the truth?" The witness attests to this promise with his hand on the Bible as he sits in the witness chair in a court of law. Why is it so important in matters of law to make sure that those testifying are telling the truth? And not just a bit of the truth, but *all* of it. Not just truth some of the time, but *all* of the time. If truth is that important in a courtroom, how much more important is it to us in our lives? There are three relationships that we need to examine to make sure we are dealing in all of the truth all of the time: ourselves, others, and God.

First, we must be honest with ourselves. Before we can be transparent with others, we must know who we are, not just who we think we are or who we want ourselves to be. We need to read God's Word and spend time with Him in prayer, asking that He reveal to us our true personalities, our true desires, and our true failings. We need help with this; we cannot do it ourselves. Even King David acknowledged his ability to deceive himself when he said, "Who can discern his errors? Forgive my hidden faults" (Psalm 19:12). Who did David think his faults were hidden from? Not God. After all, other psalms show us that David realized the all-knowing nature of God. But, David knew that he was capable of hiding his own failings from himself. If we are willing to see the truth, God will reveal to the true motivations for our actions, the times we behaved selfishly instead of lovingly, and the desires that drive us away from God instead of toward Him.

He also will help us to understand our deepest cravings. David says in a later psalm, "Delight yourself in the Lord and he will give you the desires of your heart" (Psalm 37:4).

Sometimes God fulfills desires we didn't even know we had. We receive a gift from His hand and only then realize that what He has given is a perfect fit. It satisfies us deeply. It met a need that we had not been able to see on our own.

Jesus defines Himself as truth. If we are to live in close connection to Him, we will be exposing ourselves to truth. We will begin to see things that we do not see now and will begin to understand ourselves, others, and God in the new light of truth.

TUESDAY
MEDITATION

"What you're after is truth from the inside out. Enter me, then; conceive a new, true life." (Psalm 51:6 *The Message*)

Think about the message of this verse. Acknowledge the rightness of the first sentence; then pray the second sentence to God. Spend time in His presence as He speaks truth to your soul. Write down any insights you gain.

WEDNESDAY
THOUGHTS FOR TODAY

The second area of honesty involves living truth into our relationships. Imagine that your spouse walks in and suggests that the two of you go to a particular movie that evening. You know the film and have strong feelings about not wanting to see it, but you hate to make waves. After all, you haven't been out together in a while. So you go along with the plan, but you don't enjoy the movie. Is an uneasy peace worth more to your relationship than honesty?

Sometimes we need to have enough confidence to express our own opinions and not just allow others to make decisions for us. Sometimes we need to be up front enough to talk to someone whose behavior is offensive to us. At other times, we can have the joy of speaking truth that is positive and uplifting to another person.

How do we do this? The Bible gives a great deal of help with this question in Ephesians 4:15, ". . . speaking the truth in love, we will in all things grow up into him who is the Head, that is, Christ."

The key to successful truth-speaking is love. We are told to tell the truth to each other, but truth that is told without love can be vindictive and damaging and, most likely, will be rejected. Truth and love combined will be a powerful force in building relationships, healing wounds, and enabling us all, as followers of Christ, to grow into spiritual maturity.

THURSDAY

THOUGHTS FOR TODAY

As we begin to know the truth about ourselves and put truth into practice in our relationships with others, we come to realize that *our relationship with God is the most important one in which to practice honesty*. There are reasons for this. First, He knows all about us anyway. The psalms are clear that God knows the day we were born and the day we will die. They tell of not being about to hide from God's presence or to keep secrets from Him. Jesus told us that God's knowledge of us is so vast that He even knows how many hairs are on each of our heads. If He knows all about us anyway, there is no benefit in pretense and no risk in telling Him the truth.

The second point, though, is that God loves us unconditionally and forever. Often, we are afraid that if people really knew the truth about us, they wouldn't love us. God *does* know the truth about us and He loves us anyway. There is nothing to hide and nothing to risk in being 100% honest with God.

How can we practice truthfulness with God? First, as mentioned earlier, we must let Him show us the truth about ourselves. Then, out of a heart full of light and understanding, we can express in prayer our hurt, anger, resentment, worries, desires, and requests. God's heart will respond to our hearts and the truth will set us free and give us joy.

FRIDAY

READING GOD'S MESSAGE

Ephesians 4:17-32

How is a life without truth described in verses 17-19?

Who is the source of truth referenced in verse 21?

What contrasts between truth and deceit do we see in verses 22-24?

What instructions does the writer give for relationships lived in truth? (vv. 25-32)

SATURDAY
FOR PERSONAL REFLECTION

Are there any areas in your life in which you are self-deceived?

Write down thoughts that you have and then, in a time of quiet, ask God to show you the truth about what you have written.

Know that God is gentle in His revelations and will show you only what you are ready to receive. So be patient with the process and continually over the years invite Him to be the truth-giver in your life.

Are there any relationships in which you are not entirely honest? If so, pray for guidance as you ask God to show you how to practice truth in all of the relationships in your life.

SUNDAY
PRAYER

Spirit of Truth, You are my guiding force. You have promised to guide me into all truth. This has taken away fear of being deceived. You will always tell me the truth and sort out error so I can be aware. Thank you for the gift of discernment. Keep me humble in using this gift. Don't let me mix up myself with You. You alone have the power; I get to use it, but I must remember that it is not my power. You've told me in Your Word that power belongs to God. Thank You for taking that responsibility. Help me to maintain a peaceful demeanor around difficult people, to be confident of my calling, and to choose courageous behaviors. This will keep me on the path of Truth. For me Truth is no longer a factor but a person. You are the person, Jesus, and in your name I pray. Amen

WEEK TWENTY-EIGHT

Risking Relationship

"Love is always bestowed as a gift – freely, willingly, and without expectation. We don't love to be loved. We love to love." – Leo Buscaglia

MONDAY

THOUGHTS FOR TODAY

The movie *Shadowlands* tells the story of the great love between Oxford scholar C. S. Lewis (Jack) and his American friend, Joy Davidman. As friends, they shared their love of literature, poetry, theology, and spirited discussion. Then, when Joy was about to be deported from England because her visa had expired, Jack agreed to marry her in order to allow her to stay nearby. It was a marriage in name only – Jack acknowledged their friendship, but not their love.

You get the feeling that Joy knew all along the true nature of their in-loveness. But they lived in separate homes until cancer was found in Joy's body. Then Jack suddenly realized his desperate love for her and they were married by the rector of the church and moved into Jack's country home just outside of Oxford. They had some short years together as husband and wife during which their love continued to deepen. Eventually, though, the cancer returned, and they began to prepare themselves for Joy's death. There is a quiet bedside discussion they have just before Joy dies. Jack states that he doesn't believe he can bear having her leave him. She responds that love is a package deal. The pain they will feel when she dies is part and parcel of the joy they experienced in their togetherness.

Joy dies and Jack is left to deal with his incredible grief. The account of his struggle is recorded in *A Grief Observed* in which he writes, "... for all pairs of lovers without exception, bereavement is a universal and integral part of our experience of love. It follows marriage as normally as marriage follows courtship or as autumn follows summer. It is not a truncation of the process but one of its phases; not the interruption of the dance, but the next figure" (13).

I think they would have agreed that it was worth paying the

price of grief for the great joy they experienced in their love.

Love relationships feel so good at the beginning that they offer a deceptive safeness. We feel at home with our beloved, totally accepted, totally secure. But if we love someone long enough, we will feel the pain that comes with relationship. God tells us that loving each other is worth the risk!

TUESDAY

MEDITATION

"What a man desires is unfailing love." (Proverbs 19:22)

Meditate on these words. Then allow God to show you your own desire for such love. Think further about those around you who also want to experience unfailing love. Write down any thoughts that come to your mind.

WEDNESDAY

THOUGHTS FOR TODAY

Jesus said we are to love our neighbor as we love ourselves. The apostle Paul says to live a life of love and to be united in love. John, a disciple of Jesus, commands that we walk in love. Love must have a recipient. If we are practicing the love commands in the Bible, we of course are reaching out to other people, engaging them in relationship, helping them when they need help, calling on them when we are in need of support, and committing to walk life's journey with these, our brothers and sisters in God's family.

What might it cost us to enter into such relationships? For the Good Samaritan, it cost money, time, revision of his schedule, and even the risk of ridicule. For us, it may be no less. We will sacrifice time, resources, and our own personal comforts to relate to another human being. And no matter how great the love we share with another person, hurt will come. Because we are in relationship with flawed creatures (ourselves included!), there will be acts or words that cause pain.

As Christians, we then have a choice. We can abandon the relationship that hurts and move on to one that is less demanding or we can stay and, in doing so, practice the spiritual disciplines of forgiveness, acceptance, and loyalty. If we choose the latter, we will find that the difficult relationships in our lives create opportunities for us to become more and more like Jesus.

THURSDAY
THOUGHTS FOR TODAY

How do we practice these relationship disciplines in our lives? First, we close all escape doors. If we are in a marriage, we don't even look for reasons to divorce. If we are in difficult relationships at work, at church, in the neighborhood, or in the family, we don't see flight as an out. Instead, we come face-to-face with the person we are having a problem with, we commit to working out our conflicts, and we practice whatever self-discipline and self-sacrifice it may take to reach far enough to truly connect. This is not the norm in our culture. But it is the expectation in God's kingdom.

It sounds like a lot of effort. And it is. It sounds like a lot more giving than receiving. And it is. But in our willingness to die to ourselves, we will find that our deepest needs are met. God honors those who honor His Word and engage in committed, sacrificial relationships that require setting aside of our own agendas.

That's what Jesus did for us. If our goal is to allow the nature of Jesus to be formed in us, relationships give us opportunities to do just that. When we move toward another person, we will be amazed at how God will empower us to follow through. In the end, we will agree with Joy Davidman Lewis that the joy of a committed love relationship is worth the pain that is part and parcel of the deal.

FRIDAY
READING GOD'S WORD

1 John 3:16-24

These words were written by John, who is described as the disciple for whom Jesus has a special love. No wonder John is one who writes to us about God's love for us and the kind of love we should have for others. Think about these things as you read:

Who is the great love example given in verse 16? What command is given to us in the same verse?

What example does verse 17 give about one way to show our love for another person?

Think of ways that you can show love in actions and truth as verse 18 describes.

To whom are we ultimately accountable for our lives of love? (vv. 19-20)

What reward does God give those who are obedient in relationships? (vv. 21-22)

SATURDAY
FOR PERSONAL REFLECTION

Take a few minutes to conduct a relationship inventory in your life. Are you in relationships with . . .

conflicts to be resolved?
forgiveness to be given?
reconciliation to be sought?
sacrificial love to be shown?

If so, pray, committing to God that you will do whatever it takes to reach out toward the other persons in these relationships. Pray that you will be sensitive to the Spirit's direction regarding timing, words, and attitudes. Leave the results of your efforts in God's hands. Then move forward with a soft heart and an attitude of love.

SUNDAY
PRAYER

Lord Jesus, I have a choice. I can choose safety or I can choose love.

I want love, but it is scary because love does not control, it does not demand its own way, it rejoices in the truth and in justice. Give me a 'want to', Lord. I'm helpless to love on my own; I need Your power. I humbly ask You to give me the time to love and forgive and restore and renew. If I choose to love, I let go of me and yet, Lord, you give me my real personality to become the person You created me to be. Thank you for the mystery of Your work. I don't understand it all, but I know it is good and excellent. Amen.

(13) C. S. Lewis, *A Grief Observed* (London: Faber & Faber, 1961), p. 41.

WEEK TWENTY-NINE

For the Long Haul

"Be faithful in small things because it is in them that our strength lies." – Mother Teresa

MONDAY

THOUGHTS FOR TODAY

    We are a society of quitters. Have you noticed? Pollster George Barna sure has. He says that Baby Boomers are likely to change industries (not just jobs, but career changes) a couple of times during their working years. Their children, the Busters, will probably change industries six to twelve times during their work life (14). Any how many people do we know who change churches with regularity? Barna tells us that the current younger generation has observed that "move on" behavior in their parents and, so, instead of attaching to any one church, tends to go from one church to another, perhaps being peripherally involved in three or four churches in their community all at the same time. Marriage, the "till death do us part" relationship, doesn't fare much better. Unfortunately, the divorce statistics are just as dismal for self-identified Christians as for non-Christians. What makes it so hard to hang in there when the going gets tough? What can we do to learn to be committed to one another in a way that honors God, makes us spiritually mature, and encourages others?

    At a minimum, we have to be willing to put someone else's needs ahead of our own. We have to practice what Scripture calls "self-denial." We long for comfort, for peace, and for approval. When we find that a relationship stops giving us those things, our first tendency is to bail out. Instead, God requires that we commit the relationship to Him; sacrifice our own comfort, our personal peace, and the approval of others; and look, instead, toward meeting those needs in the other person.

    Jesus is our pattern. He gave of Himself in every relationship He entered. He gave of His time, His energy, His patience, His comfort, and eventually His very life. And He is the one who gives us the instruction, "Anyone who comes with me has to let me lead.

You're not in the driver's seat – I am. Don't run from suffering; embrace it. Follow me and I'll show you how. Self-help is no help at all. Self-sacrifice is the way, *my* way, to finding yourself, your true self." (Luke 9:23-24 *The Message*).

There are challenges to maintaining long-term relationships, to be sure. People change, circumstances change, and, because we live longer than our ancestors did, there is more opportunity for those changes to disrupt the flow of relationship. God says that we are not to quit. We are to persist in doing good. We are to emulate Jesus. We are to be faithful in our committed relationships.

TUESDAY

MEDITATION

"So guard yourself in your spirit and do not break faith." (Malachi 2:16b)

Think about these words, focusing especially on guarding your spirit so you can remain faithful.

What does God reveal to you as you meditate? Write it down.

WEDNESDAY

THOUGHTS FOR TODAY

God chose the people of Israel to be His own. They were to be the keepers of the messages He gave, which have now become our Scriptures. The people of Israel were to be an example to the nations around them of how God treats with love and kindness those who are faithful to Him. And they were to be the people through whom God would send His Son to be the Savior of the world.

He showed His love to Israel in many ways. He gave them land, prospered their crops, and provided instructions for how to relate to each other and to Him. He gave them wise and able leaders and godly spiritual mentors. But Israel was not faithful to God. Over and over again, we are told of their intermarriage with idol-worshipping peoples, of their adopting the worship of other gods as part of their religion, and of their refusal to follow the instructions God had given for worship, giving, and governance.

Through it all, God was faithful. There were times when He punished Israel, times when He was silent, and times when He allowed their bad choices to bring enough chaos to drive them back to Him. But He never stopped loving them, never turned them away when they were ready to restore relationship. God's relationship to Israel, in spite of the fact that they often rejected His love, is an example of how He wants us to be faithfully committed in the one-on-one relationships in our lives.

THURSDAY
THOUGHTS FOR TODAY

How can we show the kind of commitment to each other that God showed to Israel? First, as we mentioned, *we never look for an escape**. As soon as we begin to think about ways to escape the hard realities of relationships we are in, we lose perspective. God says to persevere, to endure, and to be faithful. Long-term relationships give us an opportunity to do just that.

Second, we begin to see the other person through Jesus' eyes. If we have trouble seeing their point of view, we can ask God to show us His. When we begin to realize just how much Jesus loves the person with whom we are having so much trouble, we will begin to love him/her a little more, too, and will place far greater value in sticking with the relationship even in the tough times.

Third, we move toward the other person with softness in our heart. Maybe we can't see their point of view. We know that working through the conflict between us may be long and painful. But we move in that direction out of obedience to God's direction to be faithful to one another.

Fourth, we keep our eye on eternity. We know that this life is not all there is. We are eternal beings and justice will be served in the next life, not always in this one. When we maintain that perspective, we will be willing to sacrifice present peace and comfort for the great joy that will one day come.

---

*The exception here, of course, is if we are in an abusive relationship that threatens our physical or emotional safety. If you are in a situation like that, please seek appropriate counsel and help.

FRIDAY

READING GOD'S MESSAGE

Luke 8:1-15

What does this parable teach us about persistence in relationship with God?

What kinds of things do we have to clear away from our lives in order
to develop the roots that enable us to persevere?

How can understanding the Bible and spiritual teaching help us to remain faithful to God?

SATURDAY

FOR PERSONAL REFLECTION

Think of the long-term relationships in your life: God, marriage partner, children, friends, workmates. Are there any of these relationships in your life right now that you are tempted to run from?

Think of one way that you can move toward the person(s) with whom you are having difficulty.

Ask God to help you see the difficult person(s) in your life through Jesus' eyes of love and forgiveness. Continuing in prayer, commit to taking steps of reconciliation and renewal instead of abandoning the relationship.

Thank God for the blessing that He will grant because of your obedience and faithfulness.

SUNDAY

PRAYER

Father, You are my protector; You will not give me anything for which You have not provided Your grace which is sufficient in my weakness. You will show me how to guard my heart and how to listen to You, Holy Spirit, the Counselor. You ask me the questions that show me my heart. I can't hide from You and why would I? You ask me to sit with my doubts and fears and we look at them together. You are not shocked or reproachful. You calm me to know that there is time to handle these issues of life that spring from my heart. I will spend this time and grow into Your new life that is tailor-made for me. Thank You for dressing me in Your robe of righteousness now and forevermore. Amen.

(14) George Barna, *The Second Coming of the Church* (Nashville: Thomas Nelson, 1998), p. 63.

WEEK THIRTY

Through the Struggles

"Jesus is comfortable with broken people who remember how to love." – Brennan Manning

MONDAY
THOUGHTS FOR TODAY

We may protest against suffering, but the fact that it comes does not come as a surprise to any of us. We know that we live in a world where suffering abounds and we are not exempt. Our bodies get sick and experience pain. We have financial reverses. Our country goes to war and we or those we love are called to serve. We are asked to do things at work that we don't agree with and our stomach churns with our internal tug-of-war. But of all the struggles we experience in this life, there are probably none so difficult and so troubling as conflict between us and those with whom we are in close relationship.

When God created Adam and Eve, there was never a problem between them. They perfectly fulfilled each other's needs. They talked openly, walked with God together, and tended the garden in peace and joyfulness. But the snake entered this lovely picture, introduced sin, and, in doing so, erected great barriers to open relationships between human beings and between humans and their Creator. Adam and Eve began to hide from God, they began to blame each other for their problems, and they raised children who allowed the conflict between them to escalate to the point of murder. Don't you wish we could go back to the idyllic times of pre-sin Eden?

Some day we will. In the book of Revelation, Jesus announces that He is making all things new. The Eden first created will be restored. Relationships will be full of love and goodwill. Nations will stop warring with one another and peace will reign. Bodies will be restored as sickness and death are overcome. But we are in the in-between time now – after the sin introduced in Genesis and before the restoration promised in Revelation. How do we handle suffering and broken relationships in the in-between time of this world?

If we can see relational struggles as opportunities to grow in our walk with God, we will have a perspective that brings hope to otherwise dismal situations. Instead of seeing other persons as obstacles to get around, we can see them as a personal challenge. We can begin to want to understand them, meet their needs, and see them as Jesus sees them. We can begin to take our eyes off ourselves and our own hurts and difficulties and put them onto Jesus, Who tells us to deny ourselves and follow Him. That is the first step (and the hardest!) in the road toward spiritual maturity in our earthly relationships.

TUESDAY

MEDITATION

"The testing of your faith develops perseverance. Perseverance must finish its work so that you may be mature and complete, not lacking anything." (James 1:3b-4)

Meditate on these words from James. As God enlightens you for application of this passage to your life, write down the understanding that He gives.

WEDNESDAY

THOUGHTS FOR TODAY

If we have difficult relationships in our lives, let's not run away. Let's commit to staying and getting refocused on what God is going to do in us and through us in the middle of this difficult time. The willingness to deal with the problem relationship does a number of things for us. First, if we feel defeated and everything we have tried has failed, we are forced to rely on God. We have already learned that He wants us to be dependent on Him. There is no better place for dependence than when we feel backed into a corner with nowhere to turn. We look up. We refocus on God Who has promised never to leave us. He is there and waiting to be found.

Then, we must remember that other people are observing our times of testing. If we are having troubles in our marriage, our children are watching. We are being examples to them of what a child of God does when relationships hurt. If we are having conflict in the workplace, our fellow employees are watching.

If we are unhappy in our churches, our fellow Christians are watching. Our dealings with other people will reflect on the God we serve. He wants us to be willing to do the right thing because it is the right thing and not because we benefit personally from it. When we do that, we will grow in our dependence on God, we will be strengthened in our spirits, and glory will go to God as others watch us grow.

THURSDAY
THOUGHTS FOR TODAY

When Jesus came, He gave us a glimpse of what the world will be like when He accomplishes the restoration He has planned. Every time He healed a blind man, brought a person back from the grave, touched a leper, and held children on His lap, He was showing us what the world will be like when He takes control. We don't know when that will happen, but we do know that He left His teachings so that we could carry the message of renewal and hope to the world around us.

Every time we become an agent of reconciliation in a broken relationship, we are being used of God to bring more and more of His kingdom to this world. Satan wants destroyed relationships, separated families, conflicted churches. God is about love, peace, joy, and fulfillment. We get to choose whose agents we will be.

Every time we

- confront in love instead of walking away in anger
- seek forgiveness when we have offended
- silently let others take the credit for the good we have done
- choose not to respond to our accusers
- reach out in love to those who oppose us
- forgive even those who do not seek our good will

we are being agents of God's grace in this world. Though we cannot heal the sick and raise the dead as Jesus did, we *can* work for our Master today by bringing God's kingdom principles to bear in our relationships.

FRIDAY
READING GOD'S MESSAGE

Hebrews 12:7-17

Read this passage and then think about the following questions:

How can hardship in our lives be used as a discipline?

What is the purpose of God's discipline in our lives (v. 10)?

What does verse 12 teach us about endurance?

How will discipline show itself in our relationships (v. 14)?

How does a bitter root adversely affect our relationships (v. 15)?

How is Esau an illustration for us of persevering in difficult times in order to keep our eye on the ultimate goals God has for us (vv. 16-17)?

SATURDAY
FOR PERSONAL REFLECTION

What is the most difficult relationship in your life right now?

What are you learning as you deal with the issues between you?

Are you growing spiritually through this situation? How? Or why not?

What is one thing you can do today that will honor God in this relationship?

Sometimes it helps us to realize that everyone suffers. Think of those in your circle of acquaintance who are struggling in relationships right now. Pray that they will see God in the middle of their suffering and will persist in doing the right thing to accomplish God's will in their relationships.

SUNDAY
PRAYER

Lord Jesus, I follow You, a suffering Savior. I am to pick up my cross and follow You to Calvary and there at Calvary, my burdens are lifted. Help me not to be a shirker or to manipulate my circumstances. I let them go, content to hear You say, "Well done, thou good and faithful servant". O my soul let that be enough for me. I desire only Your approval. Lord. That will keep me free. Is it possible, Lord, to live a life of freedom in this broken, fallen world? You smile at me and say, "Yes, my child, come to Me and I will give you rest from all these questions". I am coming, Lord. Amen.

WEEK THIRTY-ONE

Learning to Forgive

"Forgiveness is the way of God. It begins along the path through pain; it stares down the perpetrator; it releases all debts. Forgiveness is the path to peace." – Seth Harris

MONDAY
THOUGHTS FOR TODAY

If you have been in any relationship for a period of time, you have experienced hurt. The nature of long-term, committed relationships is that flawed human beings are coming together in lives, spirits, and common goals. That connection creates vulnerability which makes the partners in those relationships dangerously susceptible to hurt. Because we will never see life exactly from another's viewpoint and because there is no human being who will ever love and accept us perfectly, hurt is inevitable. When it occurs, we are given the opportunity to perfect our forgiveness skills.

But as soon as we realize forgiveness is required of us, we will find that forgiveness is one of the hardest things we have ever had to do. "Forgiveness, I'm convinced, is so unnatural an act that it takes practice to perfect" (15). Some of us have had lots of practice already. Others of us need to keep at it until practice makes forgiveness flow naturally from our hearts.

There are several reasons forgiveness is so difficult. *First, we can never see any situation completely from another person's perspective.* Therefore, we have to give them lots of allowance for the fact that there may be a point of view different than our own. Giving another that latitude is very difficult.

Second, we sometimes enjoy nursing the hurts we have received. We become accustomed to licking our wounds, rehearsing the injustice in our minds, and having a focus for our anger. We don't realize how much better off we will be when we forgive the offending person and accept the healing that only forgiveness can give.

Third, we want the other person to deserve forgiveness

before we give it. If they would just apologize, recognize their wrong, desire reconciliation, or make up for the hurt they have inflicted, *then* we would be willing to forgive. The problem with this theory is that the one with an unforgiving heart is the bigger loser. If we have been hurt and we know we did not deserve that hurt, we can be healed only when we forgive the one who hurt us.

The healing we will receive is worth the gift of forgiveness we give. Remember our example: Jesus forgave those who were nailing him to the cross. They didn't ask for forgiveness; they didn't even recognize that what they were doing was wrong. Jesus forgave because forgiving is what He does. He has demonstrated the process. Now He wants us to follow in His steps.

TUESDAY

MEDITATION

"Be even-tempered, content with second place, quick to forgive an offense. Forgive as quickly and completely as the Master forgave you." (Colossians 3:13 *The Message*)

Read this verse a few times. Then focus in meditation on a phrase that the Holy Spirit highlights for you. Let the words soak into your heart. Write down any messages you may receive through your thoughts.

WEDNESDAY

THOUGHTS FOR TODAY

A great example in scripture of forgiveness is found in the book of Genesis. Joseph was sold into slavery by his older brothers who hated him because he was his father's favorite son. Years later, Joseph had risen from being a slave in Egypt to being the second most powerful person in the country. At a time of severe famine, his brothers came to Egypt to buy food and ended up in front of the very brother they had sold many years before. They didn't realize who he was, but he recognized them. You can imagine the memories brought up by seeing them! How they had hated him, put him in a pit, sold him, and told their father he was dead. Forgiving would not be easy and it didn't happen on that first visit. It took months and a several appearances in front of Joseph before he could finally tell them that he knew they intended to harm him, but he now realized that God intended to use what they did to him for a good purpose.

Forgiveness is a process. When we have experienced a hurt we did not deserve, we are angry. Once we give that anger to God, we can get to a point of knowing we need to forgive. When we express to Him our willingness to forgive, at the same time acknowledging our inability to do so, God will begin the healing process in us in order to get us to a point where forgiveness is possible. The forgiveness that comes, then, is not natural, but supernatural.

THURSDAY
THOUGHTS FOR TODAY

The Bible tells us that God remembers our sins no more (Isaiah 43:25). God, of course, knows everything, so He does not actually forget our sins. But He does say that He will not call our forgiven sins to His remembrance. Our pasts are in the record somewhere, but He's not going to look it up. It should be our goal in forgiving someone to do the same.

Again, this will be a process. As we start to heal and then we exercise the spiritual discipline of not nursing old wounds, the forgetting begins. Lewis Smedes in his book *Forgive and Forget,* says, "Once we have forgiven, we get a new freedom to forget . . The test of forgiving lies with healing the lingering pain of the past, not with forgetting that the past ever happened." (16). He goes on to explain that while we cannot forget as well as God can, what we can do is begin to feel about the offending person the way we would feel if the offense had never occurred. This softening of our heart toward the other is what often allows reconciliation between the forgiver and the forgiven to occur.

Forgiving is nothing short of a miracle. It is a miracle of grace extended by us, who have received so much grace from God already, to those who need to receive it from us. By forgiving, we become participants in the grand miracle of grace that God has put in motion in His world.

FRIDAY
READING GOD'S MESSAGE

Luke 15:11-32

How do you think each of the following characters in this story were hurt?

Father

Younger son

Elder son

How did each respond to the hurt?

What was the end result for each?

What does this parable teach about the benefits of forgiveness?

SATURDAY
FOR PERSONAL REFLECTION

Spend some time searching your heart. What hurts do you find there?

Ask God to begin the healing process so that you will someday be free of the pain of past hurts.

If someone caused your pain, you may still need to forgive that person. If that is so, tell God that you are willing to forgive if He will enable you to do so.

Thank Him for the process of forgiveness that He will take you through and the spiritual growth you will experience as a result.

SUNDAY
PRAYER

Lord, I pray that I will be willing to be made willing to forgive those who have not met my needs. My ego that wants to be right and free from any source of guilt or error needs to die and I have to choose to let it. The spirit is willing, but the flesh is weak. Please nurture my spirit, Holy Spirit, to encourage right actions, that the real me may rise to new life radiating Jesus' life of love and acceptance. In Your holy name, I pray. Amen.

(15) Gary Thomas, *Sacred Marriage* (Grand Rapids, Zondervan, 2000), p. 168
(16) Lewis Smedes, *Forgive and Forget* (New York: Pocket Books, a division of Simon & Schuster, Inc.), p. 60-61

WEEK THIRTY-TWO

Living Forgiven

"Many promising reconciliations have broken down because, while both parties came prepared to forgive, neither party came prepared to be forgiven." – Charles Williams

MONDAY
THOUGHTS FOR TODAY

We are all very aware of hurts we carry around due to the words, actions, or inactions of others. But we may not be quite as aware of the fact that sometimes we have been the cause of pain to others. We might be amazed to know how someone close to us responded internally to something we said or something we did. There may be a wound there we never intended to inflict.

Then there other choices we have made knowing full well that those choices would hurt someone else. Or we have set out intentionally to inflict hurt because we were angry or frustrated. What about the times we verbally strike back w that what we say will have a stinging impact? Because we know those close to us so well, we successfully aim at their vulnerabilities. Then we move on with our day, often never giving a second thought to the damage that our words or deeds have done.

We need to be forgiven. At some point, if we are communicating with God, the Holy Spirit will convict us about what we have done. We will realize that a sin committed against another human being is actually committed against God himself. Remember David's prayer to God after his now well-known adultery with Bathsheba? "Against you, you only, have I sinned and done what is evil in your sight" (Psalm 51:4a).

Wait a minute, you say, what choice did Bathsheba have in this matter? He was the king so she really couldn't say no to him without risking her life. Didn't David sin against Bathsheba? And what about her husband Uriah? First David impregnated his wife and then had him killed on the front lines of battle. Weren't those sins against Uriah? Yes, David caused incredible hurt in the lives of Uriah and Bathsheba, but at the end of the day, he realized that, at the core, his sin was against the holy God.

We know the same thing. There are people we have treated unfairly and have hurt deeply. We need their forgiveness to be sure. But our even greater need is to acknowledge our sinfulness before the God of heaven who is so holy that He cannot look upon sin. Once we see that, we go to God in repentance, relying on His promise to forgive those who acknowledge their sin and seek his face. As David states it, "A broken and contrite heart, O God, you will not despise" (Psalm 51:17b).

TUESDAY

MEDITATION

"You are forgiving and good, O Lord, abounding in love to all who call to you." (Psalm 86:5)

Meditate on these words as you pray them to the Lord. Allow the Spirit to enlighten you as to the meaning of this verse to you today. Write any thoughts that come to your mind.

WEDNESDAY

THOUGHTS FOR TODAY

What do you do when someone offers you the gift of forgiveness? If we know we need it, we are usually able to accept it with thanksgiving. But if we haven't yet acknowledged our guilt, receiving forgiveness can be humbling experience. We may find it far easier to be the magnanimous forgiver than it is to be the one who is in the position of needing forgiveness.

Remember, we may not be aware of offenses we have caused. If someone is hurt by what we have done, we do not need to argue them out of the hurt. Once we become aware of such a situation, we must simply acknowledge their pain and accept the forgiveness they offer with thankfulness that they are willing to deal with the issue between us and restore our relationship. If we know we have offended and seek forgiveness, there is even more reason to be happy when it is freely given. Going through the process of acknowledging offense and accepting forgiveness leaves us with a relationship be happy when it is freely given. Going through the process of acknowledging offense and accepting forgiveness leaves us with a relationship that is stronger and better than ever before. Not only is the slate of offenses wiped clean, but the reconciliation enables us to realize how much we valued the relationship in the first place.

If that is true on a human level, how much more so in our relationship with God! Jesus once told His disciples that the degree of our love for Him has a great deal to do with the amount of forgiveness we have received. Think about that. God's forgiveness draws us closer to Him in love, dependence, and gratefulness.

THURSDAY
THOUGHTS FOR TODAY

The really great thing about God's forgiveness is that we can live right in the middle of it all the time. We will sin, to be sure, but God has promised forgiveness for every sin that we have ever committed and ever sin that we will commit. We simply acknowledge that what we have done is sinful, that it is an offense to God, and that we would rather please Him than hurt Him. He forgives, not because we deserve it, but because Jesus paid the price so that forgiveness could be ours.

In fact, if we could peek into heaven today, we might see an interesting scene. We might see Satan standing in the presence of God and suddenly you hear your name come from his mouth. He says you are a fraud, you are not being completely honest in your dealings with others. God turns to Jesus to see His response and Jesus quietly, but firmly, says, "I've got it covered. I paid for that."

Can we see why forgiveness is so important to God? He is holy and perfect and we cannot meet His standards. We need forgiveness daily and it is provided through Jesus Christ. And now that we are living forgiven, we see how it is possible for us to forgive others. The offenses committed against us are nothing compared to those we have committed (and even continue to commit) against God. If He can forgive us, He can also enable us to forgive others. And He does.

FRIDAY

READING GOD'S MESSAGE

Matthew 6:9-15

How is our forgiveness by God and our forgiveness of others tied together in The Lord's Prayer?

What explanation does Jesus give in verses 14 and 15?

Why do you suppose that, of all the sentences in The Lord's Prayer, Jesus chose to take one and explain it more thoroughly?

What characteristics are required in order to pray each of the sentences of this prayer with sincerity?

SATURDAY

FOR PERSONAL REFLECTION

Do a heart check today.

Do you carry guilt? What is the remedy? Is there anything that keeps you from going to God in confession so you can live forgiven?

Do you carry resentment or bitterness? What is the remedy? Is there anything that keeps you from offering the grace of forgiveness to another person?

Imagine what your life would be like without guilt, resentment, or bitterness. Pray, asking God to lead you in the steps to getting there.

SUNDAY

PRAYER

Lord, you know that I have carried bitterness, resentment and unforgiveness in my heart and have had to spend time with these tormentors. It was not a fun time. Again, You had to forgive me for my ignorance and unbelief. You really do mean what You say in your Word. O how lovingly You have worked with me to show how to let go of the debts I was holding against others. You are such a thorough trainer and a thorough lover. Jesus, lover of my soul, I love You. Amen.

WEEK THIRTY-THREE

The Difference God Makes

"The quality of a godly life does not depend on its number of great happenings or big actions, but on what happens in it one small moment after another." – Leonard Sweet

MONDAY

THOUGHTS FOR TODAY

Nobody should be able to do relationships better than Christians. We are forgiven, so we can forgive. We are filled with the Holy Spirit so we have power to choose to do right and to say "no" to wrong. We are given the mind of Christ, so we have supernatural wisdom and discernment in understanding ourselves and others. We have the perfect example in Jesus who lived a life of love among some fairly unlovable people. And we are given specific instructions concerning how to treat each other.

With all those advantages, why do Christians seem to have as many marriage problems as non-Christians? Why is there in-fighting in churches to the extent that splits occur? Why do Christian businessmen find themselves in court asking the judge to decide between them? Why do Christian parents struggle in dealing with rebellious children?

Maybe it could be a little bit better if we were able to view relationships in the right way. Sometimes we see others as being put into our lives to enrich us, to make us happy, to meet our needs, and to fulfill us in some way. People get married for those reasons. They choose to have babies for those reasons. And they make choices concerning work and church for many of the same reasons. What if we discover that these are not the reasons for relationship? What if God designed relationships "to make us holy more than to make us happy"? (17)

We are told that God's ultimate goal for us is to be like Jesus. We all have a long way to go. And instead of having all the time we want for feeding the spiritual life, we find that we are dealing with the nitty-gritty of everyday issues: getting the kids to school, figuring out how to handle finances, having sometimes too-heated discussions with our spouses, dealing with aging parents, and trying to undo the damage caused by the person who used to be a friend. But, look again.

Maybe each of these relationship issues is a training ground designed to help us develop the characteristics that God wants us to have. Maybe each problem is a signpost directing us to dependence on God for guidance and wisdom. Maybe there are, after all, some changes we need to make in our lives to be more like Christ and the relationships in which we find ourselves are the sacred school in which we learn.

TUESDAY

MEDITATION

"...**take on an entirely new way of life – a God-fashioned life, a life renewed from the inside and working itself into your conduct as God accurately reproduces his character in you.**" (Ephesians 4:24 *The Message*)

Think about this command and then quietly allow God to show you what God's character looks like when it is lived out in your life. Make some notes as you meditate in God's presence.

WEDNESDAY

THOUGHTS FOR TODAY

If relationships are God's school to help us grow into His likeness, how should we respond to significant people in our lives? The writings of Paul give us some good insights. First, we are told in Ephesians 4 to speak honestly with one another. We should always be people of the truth. We should not have hidden agendas, put up false pretenses, or be manipulative. In the same passage, Paul tells us that the truth we speak should always be presented with love.

Remember when your mother used to tell you, "If you can't say anything good, don't say anything at all"? God says it differently. Essentially, He says, "If you can't say something in love, wait until you can." As we saw in our study a few weeks ago, love and truth go together when we are dealing with others.

Just think of the spiritual character traits we can develop in learning to speak the truth in love. First, we would either have to begin to think of the problem people in our lives more lovingly or we would have to keep quiet. Before we speak to them, we would have to ask two questions: Is what I am about to say honest? Is it loving? Just slowing down to think about the other person and then to think about the consequences of our speech will make us more deliberate in approaching relationship issues. Over time we will find that we are treating others more as Jesus would.

THURSDAY — *THOUGHTS FOR TODAY*

Another relationship teaching that Paul gives in Ephesians is that of submission. We are to be willing to submit to each other. Have you have tried it? It's hard! It's difficult enough to submit to God Whom we know loves us and has our best interest at heart always. It's many times harder to submit to another human being whose motives we may not totally trust. Yet, in God's school of holiness, submission is the main teaching.

Long-term committed relationships are the laboratory in which we test our ability to submit. How are we doing? Are we learning not to always insist that our way is the right way? Are we able to put another's needs or tastes or desires ahead of our own? If we struggle in this area, we can ask God to help us recognize the next time we have an opportunity to practice submission. As we submit in little things, our submission quotient will increase and we will find ourselves submitting to others and to God in bigger things as well. In doing so, the character of Christ will be forming in us.

Jesus was willing to submit to God, the Father, in coming to earth to live among us and to offer Himself as the sacrifice for our sins. His life is the epitome of submission. If we are to be like Him, we learn to practice submission in much smaller ways, but each time we do, we are living out the example of Christ.

FRIDAY — *READING GOD'S MESSAGE*

Ephesians 5:1-6:9

In describing the life of a Christian in relationship with others, what kinds of behavior does Paul say we should get rid of?

What command is given in verses 10 and 17?

How should husbands and wives treat each other?

How should parents treat their children?

How should children treat their parents?

What commands are given for employers and employees (masters and slaves)?

SATURDAY
FOR PERSONAL REFLECTION

What character or personality issues are sometimes problematic for you?

    Spinning the truth?

    Harshness?

    Non-reliability?

    Negative attitude?

    Addiction?
    Unforgiveness?

    Bitterness?

    Hopelessness?

    Other?

Remember God, in love, wants you to become more like Jesus.

Think about how relationships in your life might be used of God to root out the issue or issues you most struggle with and free you to live as God intends. Commit your relationships to God asking Him to show you how you can redirect your thoughts to learn, through interaction with people around you, what it means to live like Christ.

SUNDAY
PRAYER

O Redeemer, my Redeemer, continue to draw me back to You when I stray off the path of life. How can having my own way seem so attractive to me? Show me, Holy Spirit, how to let go of my rights even when I'm right. In Your kingdom there is a higher law than fairness----it is love and obedience to the truth. You are the truth, Jesus, a mystery that is approachable but not understandable. I praise you for this, Father, Son, and Holy Spirit. Amen.

(17) Gary Thomas, *Sacred Marriage*, op. cit., cover.

WEEK THIRTY-FOUR

Knowing God as Spirit

"Those in whom the Spirit comes to live are God's new Temple. They are, individually, and corporately, places where heaven and earth meet." – N. T. Wright

MONDAY
                    THOUGHTS FOR TODAY

    We concluded our study on relationships with a thought about allowing difficult situations in life to shape us into the people God wants us to be. Over the next few weeks, we will look at the Holy Spirit's role in this shaping process as He brings about changes in us. First, we will look at the Holy Spirit Himself.

    Have you ever had someone say to you, "I can't come to your party, but I will be with you in spirit"? We put that statement through our mental processing and conclude that the person's body will not be there eating our food and drinking our punch, but he will be thinking of the event and would like very much to be there. We also know that the absent person's spirit will be very much connected to his body. If he is not there in body, he is really not there in spirit either.

    With God things are different. God's Spirit can be where God's body is not. Jesus came to earth, as we have seen, to take on a human form and show us, to the extent possible, what God is like. When Jesus left, He took his body with Him back to heaven, but He sent, as He had promised, His Spirit to live among us. When Jesus says, "I will be with you in Spirit," He means it literally. We are told that, once we accept the invitation to become a child of God, the Holy Spirit lives within us.

    We have our own spirits, don't we? We think of our spirits as being the essence of our true selves. While our earthly bodies will die, our spirits will live on forever. The problem with our spirits is that they are flawed. Even Adam and Eve, in the perfection of the Garden of Eden, found that they did not make a holy choice. If they couldn't bring themselves to do the right thing in the most perfect of circumstances, we know that we cannot make good and right choices living, as we do, in a fallen world. But the Spirit of God enters the picture and takes up residence within us. Then, we are told, that God's Spirit talks to our spirit and teaches us right from wrong, makes us purer, and enables us to make right and good decisions. With the indwelling Spirit of Jesus, we have the ability to choose God for now and forever. The Holy Spirit within us is greater than the power of the world around us and greater than our tendency to make wrong choices.

The Spirit is 100% God and He is our companion. He communicates His will to us, enlightens our minds to understand the Bible, and relates to us as a person. He is God's very personality living and breathing inside us!

TUESDAY

MEDITATION

"The amazing grace of the Master, Jesus Christ, the extravagant love of God, the intimate friendship of the Holy Spirit, be with all of you." (2 Corinthians 13:14 *The Message*)

Mediate on this verse focusing particularly on the "intimate friendship of the Holy Spirit." What does that mean to you? Ask for enlightenment to understand better your relationship to the Holy Spirit. Write down insights that you are given.

WEDNESDAY

THOUGHTS FOR TODAY

One of the roles of the Spirit, as we have seen, is to enable us to make right decisions. When we are born into God's family, we are given new life, and someday we will be like our older brother, Jesus. But, for now, we struggle with bad habits, sinful desires, and weak wills. One of the jobs of the Spirit is to purify our lives so that, over time we become more like Christ.

One way he does that is by *convicting us of sin.* When we make a bad choice, we feel guilty. This is not the false guilt that other people or Satan sometimes try to put upon us. This is real guilt, brought about because we have done something offensive to God's holiness. The purpose of the conviction of the Spirit is not to make us feel bad, but to bring us to a point of confession and repentance so we can be made pure again.

The second way the Spirit changes us is by *empowering us to make good choices*. As we begin to rely on the Spirit, we find that, because of His conviction, power, and love, we are growing in purity and becoming closer to being like Christ. Over time we realize the unwavering love of God and, out of gratitude, we begin to make decisions that are more honoring to Him.

THURSDAY
THOUGHTS FOR TODAY

The Spirit of God within us has roles other than making us purer. For example, He also is the one who *reveals truth to us through the Word of God*. We are told that He inspired the people who wrote the Bible (2 Peter 1:21). The Bible is the Spirit's book. Who better to be able to interpret the message of a book than the one who wrote it? We rely on the Holy Spirit to illuminate Scripture as we read it and to make it real and understandable to our hearts.

He also is known as a *prayer-carrier*. We are told (Romans 8:26-27) that the Spirit hears our prayers, translates them into what they should be, and then presents them to God for us. He intercedes for us much as a lawyer intercedes for a client. Because of the work of the Spirit, we cannot pray a bad prayer. He makes our flawed prayers into what they should be before they reach the throne of God.

The Spirit is also our *comforter and friend*. He provides strength when we are weak, defense when we are attacked, encouragement when we are down, and consolation when we are sad. Without the work of the Spirit, our Christianity would be empty form and meaningless ritual. The Spirit keeps our relationship with God alive, purposeful, and growing. He gives us the power to change internally, to relate to people outwardly, and to share the good news of Jesus with those around us.

FRIDAY

READING GOD'S MESSAGE

1 Corinthians 2:9-16

What does the Spirit reveal to us? (v.8)

Who knows God's thoughts? (v.11)

What does the Spirit help us to understand? (v.12)

Why is the Spirit's work important in helping us to understand spiritual things? (v.14)

How can we have the mind of Christ? (v.16)

As you think about the ways the Spirit of God provides for your understanding, your connection with God the Father, and the revelation of truth, how does it make you feel?

Tell God about it.

SATURDAY
FOR PERSONAL REFLECTION

As you think about this week's study, what roles of the Spirit do you most relate to?

In what ways do you need to expand your participation in the Spirit's work in your life?

Is it your desire to become holier? Why or why not? How can the Spirit help?
Is it your desire to know God better? How can the Spirit help?

Is it your desire to understand more about the Bible? How can the Spirit help?

Is it your desire to share Jesus with others? How can the Spirit help?

Spend some time in prayer, asking the Spirit, to show you the areas in which you need to trust Him more and submit to Him more completely. Then ask Him to give you the will and the power to do so.

SUNDAY
PRAYER

Holy Spirit, soul of my soul, it's such a joy to know and hear Your voice speaking to my spirit. t brings beauty to everything. I choose to let go of any resistance to Your guidance and Your love. You are trustworthy and have only my best interest at heart. Thank You for Your ministry of conviction and reconciliation. I promise to submit to whatever You permit to happen to me today, only show me what is Your will. I ask in Jesus' holy, majestic name. Amen.

WEEK THIRTY-FIVE

Connecting with the Spirit

"The more your heart is like Christ's, the more you will want the things he wants. Things that please Christ will please you." – Henry Blackaby

MONDAY
THOUGHTS FOR TODAY

As the Spirit begins to change us, He causes new character traits to grow within us. We become people we never thought we could be. We are told that these characteristics include love, joy, peace, patience, kindness, goodness, faithfulness, gentleness, and self-control (Galatians 5:22). These traits deal with our emotions, our attitudes, and our character. In other words, when the Spirit is in control, we become better people.

It is important for us to see that this change does not come as a result of our efforts to change. There are many self-improvement instructions on the shelves of our bookstores that show us how to control our tempers, heal wounded emotions, and become more lovable. That is not what this list is about. The characteristics shown in this verse are called the fruit of the Spirit for a reason. Do you know any apple, peach, or grape that gets bigger and juicier because it tries harder? No. It grows to become mature, ripened fruit simply by hanging onto the tree, bush, or vine to which it is attached.

The same principle applies to the fruit of the Spirit. We develop these characteristics in our lives simply by *cooperating with that the Spirit is doing within us.* Earlier in Galatians, Paul says, "Are you so foolish? After beginning with the Spirit, are you now trying to attain your goal by human effort?" (Galatians 3:3). There is nothing that will rob us of the joy of our relationship with God like trying to be good. We will be frustrated and angry much of the time if we do. If we want joy, we must believe God when He says He will make us like Jesus. We begin our spiritual lives when the Spirit takes up residence within us. We grow into beings who are more like Jesus by allowing the Spirit to convict, empower, and guide us. We cannot become God's children by effort, nor can we become better people by effort.

While we do not have to take the responsibility for changing ourselves, we must have the *intention to change*. We do need to learn to cooperate with the work of the Spirit in our lives. We are told many times in Scripture that change comes first of all through our minds. We must set our minds on things above (Colossians 3:2), be changed by the renewing of our minds (Romans 12:2), and focus our minds on what the Spirit desires (Romans 8:5). We point our minds and our thoughts toward God, we allow the Spirit to control, and change is guaranteed. And it will be good!

TUESDAY

MEDITATION

"I want you woven into a tapestry of love, in touch with everything there is to know of God. Then you will have minds confident and at rest, focused on Christ, God's great mystery." (Colossians 2:2 *The Message*)

Before you meditate on these words, invite the Spirit to bring His light to this message and to enable you to focus on Christ with a confident, restful mind. Write what you understand.

WEDNESDAY

THOUGHTS FOR TODAY

Spiritual growth, then, comes, not through human effort; but human willingness is required in order for it to happen. God has provided ways by which we can attach to Him and, in doing so, be connected to the power that will enable our growth. Those ways include Bible study and prayer.

The Bible is God's revealed truth to us. With the Spirit's illumination, it comes alive as we read. We need to read this book, not just for intellectual knowledge, but for understanding and application to our lives. As we read, we ask the Holy Spirit to be our teacher. He promised He would show us all truth and God is truth. So we read the Bible in gulps sometimes – whole books or multiple chapters, trying to get an overview of God's working with people,

His patterns, and His character. Then, at times, we dig in a little deeper. We check out cross references, Bible notes, or commentaries. We work to understand the context of a passage. At other times, we may find just one verse and meditate on it all day allowing its truth to sink deep into our souls.

As much as we are able, we also should memorize Bible verses or passages. Once we have them in our minds, the Spirit can bring them to our consciousness when they are most needed. Over time, we will become more familiar with God's truth and it will begin to change us when we least expect it.

THURSDAY
THOUGHTS FOR TODAY

We also can connect to God through prayer. *We engage in private times of prayer in which we sincerely seek God.* We tell Him our heart's desires, we ask that He increase our love for Him, we listen for His response and His direction to us, we obey when we feel the nudging of the Spirit, we thank Him for His care for us, and we ask that He change us to be the people He wants us to be. All of this requires a vital dependence on the Spirit who intercedes for us with the Father so that our requests can be granted.

We also find others of like mind with whom we can pray together. There is both joy and strength in corporate prayers. There is an accountability to one another, a united presentation to God, and a solidarity of purpose that brings down the power of heaven through the working of the Spirit.

One other thing we have to do in order to attach effectively to God: *We have to detach from the encumbrances of this world.* We let go of bondage to sin and bad habits in order to gain freedom. We let go of lies to know truth. We let go of outward appearances to gain inward wholeness. We let go of anger and fear to gain peace. Likeness to God is guaranteed to those who detach from this world and, instead, attach to Him and allow the Spirit to accomplish His supernatural work.

FRIDAY
READING GOD'S MESSAGE

Psalm 1

How does the man in this psalm show that he is intentional about his spiritual growth?

What is his main focus?

What kinds of companions does he avoid?

What promises are given to a person of this kind of focus? (verses 3 and 6)

Why do you suppose the psalm writer uses a tree in this analogy? How does the picture of a tree help us to understand the nature of spiritual growth?

Are you sometimes impatient with your progress spiritually? If so, tell God. Renew your intention to detach to whatever holds you back and to attach solely and completely to God through the power of the Spirit.

SATURDAY
FOR PERSONAL REFLECTION

On a scale of 1 to 10, how would you rate your Bible study habits?

What is one Bible study method you can begin today that will start you on a path to knowing more about God's word?

On a scale of 1 to 10, how would you rate your prayer life?

What new prayer commitment can you make today that will improve that rating over the next few months?

On a scale of 1 to 10, how would you rate your desire to develop an intimate relationship with God?

Pray, asking God to give you an ever-increasing desire to know Him. Make note of any response He may give back to you. Be sure to follow any direction He gives.

SUNDAY
PRAYER

Almighty God, heavenly Father, You have done what I could never do---You changed me. I looked for the old me and that person was gone. You gave me Your humility since You showed me that I have none of my own. With this insight and revelation, the freedom to be real and genuine has come, and the peace to help me keep my mind and my heart in Christ Jesus. Now You are helping me, Holy Spirit, to practice this newness on a daily basis---one day at a time. You are all I need, Jesus. I stand on this truth in Your name. Amen.

WEEK THIRTY-SIX

A Genuine Love

"Faith makes all things possible . . . love makes all things easy." –
Dwight L. Moody

MONDAY   *THOUGHTS FOR TOD0AY*

Over the next few weeks we will look at the characteristics of a Spirit controlled person: One filled with love, joy, peace, patience, kindness, goodness, faithfulness, gentleness, and self-control (Galatians 5:22). We all agree that these are good traits that we would like to show more of in our lives. We can work at being more loving, more peaceful, more faithful, and gentler, but we will fail if we do it by will power alone. We need the Spirit to change us from the inside out so that, by yielding to His control, we begin to find these characteristics developing in our lives. Growing the fruit of the Spirit in our lives is a cooperative effort between us and God.

The Spirit knows that we can't give love until we experience love. We cannot be faithful until we see a perfect example of faithfulness in our lives. We cannot foster peaceful relationships until we have internal peace. So, we find that, in growing within us the characteristics that God wants us to have, He starts by showing that characteristic toward us so we experience it firsthand. He fills us up so we can live out what He puts in.

The first evidence of the Spirit's working in our hearts is love. Once we have experienced God's love for us, we find it easier to love Him back *and* to love others around us. How would we describe the special love God has for us?

- He did not accidentally fall in love, rather, He *decided* to love us. He chose to make us His own before we were even born (Ephesians 1:4).

- God's love for us has as its *purpose* our knowing and enjoying Him. He doesn't love us as objects, rather, He wants to be in relationship with us (Isaiah 62:5).

- God's love for us is *unconditional*. It is not based on our merit, behavior, or response. It is entirely initiated and sustained by God (Romans 5:8).

- God's love is *transforming*. He heals our emotional wounds and opens our hearts to receive more and more of the love that He sends (Ephesians 3:18).

That love is there for us. We just have to be open to receive it. We do that by centering our soul, our minds, our emotions, and our energy on Him and enjoying the love He pours into us. When we are full to the brim, the fruit of love begins to show in our lives. We won't be able to hold ourselves back from being more loving toward those around us!

TUESDAY

MEDITATION

"The Lord delights in those who fear him, who put their hope in his unfailing love." (Psalm 147:11)

Meditate on these words sensing the Lord's delight in you and allowing your heart to experience His love. Write down thoughts that come to your mind or emotions that touch your heart.

WEDNESDAY

THOUGHTS FOR TODAY

It takes some time and some practice to allow the love of God to sink deep within us, but once we do, we will turn around and show that same love to others. We will find that we accept things in others that were not so acceptable to us before God showed us how to love even the unlovable. One reason we will be able to *accept others* (without asking them to change to deserve our love) is that we recognize that God is in the people-changing business so we don't *have* to be! What a relief! We can focus on our relationship with God and let the Spirit take care of changing those around us who need to be changed. We can love them as they are without have the responsibility of causing them to grow or change.

This also means that people don't have to be like us for us to show love to them. The Parable of the Good Samaritan, which we looked at earlier, is a great example of a man who showed compassion for someone who was from a society which had historically mistreated and looked down upon the Samaritans. The Good Samaritan seemed to have no problem loving someone who had not earned his love and someone who was different from himself. The injured Jew was not required to change so he could deserve the love of the Samaritan. Love that accepts the other is evidence of the working of the Spirit in our lives.

THURSDAY
THOUGHTS FOR TODAY

Another characteristic of God-like love in our hearts is *forgiveness*. Jesus once said that those who are forgiven much love much. He saw forgiveness and love as going hand-in-hand. In our love for others, we need to be willing to forgive as Christ forgave us (Colossians 3:13). Before we were lovable, before we were perfect, before we were all cleaned up and connecting to God, Jesus died to bring us forgiveness. The more we allow the Spirit to control us, the more forgiving we will be toward those who have wronged us.

Another part of love as the Spirit reveals it to us is *giving*. True love gives. Think about it. When you are in love, you want to buy gifts, you want to cook dinners, you want to show your love in tangible ways. The true love grown within us by the Spirit will do the same. We will see those around us who are in need and give to them. We will give up our place in line, we will give of our time, we will give of our money, we will share our homes, and we will open our hearts. Love and giving go hand-in-hand, too!

One more thought: If God is going to test our ability to love, He will probably not do so with someone who is just like us. He may send someone difficult to accept, to give to, and to forgive. Someone unlovable by worldly standards. Will we pass the test?

FRIDAY
READING GOD'S MESSAGE

1 Corinthians 13

What does the writer convey in the first three verses about the overriding importance of love?

What are the positive things that define love in verse 4?

What are we told that love is *not* in verse 5?

What positive actions does love take in verses 6 and 7?

Whom will we see face to face as implied in verse 12? What will we know better then than we know now?

Why do you think that love identified as the greatest of all virtues?

SATURDAY
FOR PESONAL REFLECTION

How do you define love?

Is your definition consistent with God's in the chapter you read yesterday?

Is love growing as a fruit of the Spirit in your life? How do you know?

Spend some time in prayer and -

- ask God to show you how you can show more love in the way you live your life.

- ask Him to put opportunities in front of you this week to choose love instead of apathy or anger or dislike or hate.

- invite Him to show you attitudes or activities you may need to change in order to create a more favorable environment in your heart for love to grow. Write down any thoughts or direction that He gives.

SUNDAY

PRAYER

Father, you are the God of the impossible. There is always hope because You are alive. Jesus, You are alive! You are not only alive but You love me and are available 24/7. All I need do is call on You, to say Your name, and You are there to show me my needs, meet my needs and hold my hand while I wait on Your timing. I don't know what's good for me, but You will show me when I am ready to receive. Thank You for Your patience. I want more of Your patience. In faith, I receive it. I love you. Amen.

WEEK THIRTY-SEVEN

A Bubbling Up Joy

"A Christian should be an Alleluia from head to foot!" – St. Augustine

MONDAY

THOUGHTS FOR TODAY

Did you ever think of joy as a responsibility? As followers of God, it is His desire for us to be joyful and to be joy-spreaders in this world around us. Joy is not for a chosen few, it is for everyone. Yet, as we think of the people in our lives right now who are not experiencing joy, we realize that we are surrounded by pain, sorrow, depression, and sadness. I have a friend who cried uncontrollably for two weeks while doctors and counselors tried to help with advice and medication. I have a sister-in-law who is recovering from painful hand surgery, a long-term associate just diagnosed with bone cancer and having to give up her business, a friend who is a mother struggling to make ends meet with six children and no husband, and another friend who continues in a difficult marriage though there are conflicts on an almost daily basis.

Where is the joy?

Jesus prayed that we, as His followers, would have His joy made complete within us (John 17:13). Has God not answered His own Son's prayer? I believe He has responded, but maybe we have not been receptive to the answer. If God wants us to have joy, why don't we? I think it is, in part, because we have not chosen joy. Too often we choose to focus on the problem, and not on Jesus, who can solve the problem. We focus on the pain, and not on the Spirit who is the comforter in our pain. We focus on the conflict and not on the one who came to this world to bring peace.

We are commanded in Scripture to be joyful always (Philippians 4:4). We would not be told to be joyful in all things if it were not possible to do so. This tells us, doesn't it, that the joy the Bible speaks of is not dependent upon the circumstances of our lives? In fact, a study at the University of California concluded that only 10% of the happiness people feel is circumstantial. The rest is based on mindset, attitude, and choice.

We are ambassadors of a joy-filled God. If we are not experiencing that joy, we are not representing Him well. Joy is both a responsibility and a privilege. It also has a purpose: The purpose is to give us strength for this life (Nehemiah 8:10). Joy is our energizer, our resilience, and our power. Choosing joy will strengthen us for all of life's ups and downs. But how?

TUESDAY

MEDITATION

"**. . . weeping may remain for a night, but rejoicing comes in the morning.**" (Psalm 30:5b)

Meditate on the words of this verse and then claim it as a promise concerning any difficult circumstances you face right now. Eventually morning will come and joy will be there with it. Think on these things.

WEDNESDAY

THOUGHTS FOR TODAY

If we are choosing to be joyful and still are not experiencing it, we have to stop to see what is blocking the joy God wants to send our way. *The first block may be sin.* If we have sinful attitudes such as envy, resentment, critical spirit, or unforgiveness, joy cannot get through. And, sinful actions, though they may bring temporary enjoyment, will not bring *true* joy. Instead, sin leads to despair and hopelessness. So the first step toward joy is confession. That step of obedience might lead us initially through a path of suffering, but at the end of that path is joy. Once we realize that we have been living in disobedience, we simply acknowledge that fact before God and ask for His forgiveness and cleansing. Joy will pour over us! I've seen it happen.

A second block to joy may be our own selves. If we are living lives in our own strength, we will burn out. We can do only so many good deeds and accomplish only so many spiritual milestones before we get tired. The sooner we give up trying so hard and give ourselves, as we are, over to God, the quicker the joy can come. When we have given control to God, we find that, no matter what is going on in our lives, we are resting secure in the One who is powerful and good and will see us through. Joy becomes our auto pilot through every kind of stress.

THURSDAY
THOUGHTS FOR TODAY

British writer George MacDonald is credited with saying there are three things we need to make us joyful: someone to love, something to do, and something to hope for. Through our relationship in Christ, we have all three.

First, we have someone to love. We know that only God is worthy of our fullest love and deepest devotion. In fact, if God were the only One we ever loved, it would be enough. "Whom have I in heaven but you? And earth has nothing I desire besides you." (Psalm 73:25). Our love for God empowers and motivates everything else we do. But in our lives as Christians, God has given us the joy of loving each other, too. There is no bond so deep as the bond between two people who both love God completely.

Second, we have something to do. The activities we engage in as God's children are purposeful. He wants us to do what we do with all our might and to the best of our ability. He wants us to bring the message of His kingdom to earth. Knowing that all that we do on earth has an eternal consequence gives our lives real purpose.

Third, we have something to hope for. In this life we have hope because we know we can trust the God who is in control. But there is more to our hope than what we see in this life. We know there is a promised life to come in which we will experience joy to the full and forever!

FRIDAY
READING GOD'S MESSAGE

John 11:1-44

Describe the situation Jesus came into as He entered Bethany.

How did Mary feel?

How did Martha feel?

How did Jesus feel?

How do you suppose those feelings changed after Lazarus came out of the grave alive?

In your opinion, was it worth going through their grief in order to experience the joy at seeing their brother raised? Why or why not?

SATURDAY
FOR PERSONAL REFLECTION

Think about a time in your life when all seemed to be going wrong, but joy was the end result of the problem. How does that story increase your faith in God?

Which of these three areas do you need to focus on in order to experience more joy in your life?

- Someone to love
- Something to do
- Something to hope for

Pray, asking God to show you the next step as you seek to please Him in that area of your life. Write down anything that He may reveal to you.

SUNDAY
PRAYER

Lord, I want to offer You a sacrifice of praise. I choose to praise You for not taking away the pain in my life but showing me how to walk through it with You at my side. You made the Word take on flesh when You said, "Even when the way goes through Death Valley, I'm not afraid when You walk at my side, Your trusty shepherd's crook makes me feel secure" (Psalm 23:4 The Message). I admit that, at first, I was afraid but, with Your grace to help me take the first step, came the courage to keep going through the pain of looking in the mirror and seeing what I didn't want anymore. Seeing my helplessness to get rid of the sin in my life gave me the power to ask You to remove it and exchange it for Your life, Jesus. That is why You died, so I could have Your life and, in that way, discover my real personality reflected from Your face. What wondrous love is this, O my soul, O my soul? What wondrous love is this, O my soul? Amen.

WEEK THIRTY-EIGHT

Invitation to Peace

"If God be our God, He will give us peace in trouble. When there is a storm without, He will make peace within. The world can create trouble in peace, but God can create peace in trouble". – Thomas Watson

MONDAY

THOUGHTS FOR TODAY

The Hebrew word translated as *peace* in our English Bibles is *shalom*. We have all heard that term in movies, in books, or among our Jewish friends. The meaning of *shalom* is broader than the word used for peace in our English language. It "carries a greater connotation of well-being, health, safety, prosperity, wholeness, and completeness." (18) . Let's keep the broader significance of that meaning in mind as we look today at three arenas in which God wants His *shalom* to show itself in our lives.

First, we desire and require *peace with God*. We know that sin separates us from God so that, instead of experiencing His *shalom*, we feel fear, anxiety, and isolation, just as Adam and Eve experienced when they were hiding in the garden. But, thankfully, we are told in Scripture that we can have peace with God through the payment that Jesus made for our sins. As long as we keep turning ourselves and our hearts toward God, we are assured that we will have peace with Him. In many ways, with that all-encompassing relationship in place, everything else in our lives becomes of secondary importance.

But many of us long for *peace within ourselves*. We yearn for the *shalom* of God that includes an overall sense of well-being. Once we are reconciled to God through Jesus, experiencing internal peace is simply a matter of trusting Him. Jesus taught His disciples that, in spite of the problems they would have in this world, they could live in his *shalom* because He was greater than this world and greater than their problems. They just needed to trust in His overcoming power. The same message is true for us today.

We also want to live at *peace with one another*. We don't

like war, we don't like quarrels, and we don't like living in tension with other people. God doesn't like these things either. In fact, we are told, "If it is possible, as far as it depends on you, live at peace with everyone" (Romans 12:18). While internal peace requires trust in God, peace with one another requires humility. We will have peace to the extent that we are willing to put ourselves in second place and, instead of valuing being right, we seek the higher value of peace. God will honor the man or woman who puts His values ahead of their own.

TUESDAY

MEDITATION

"Peace I leave with you; my peace I give you. I do not give to you as the world gives. Do not let your hearts be troubled and do not be afraid." (John 14:27)

Think about this promise and this command. As you meditate on the words, allow the Spirit to speak words of peace and well-being to your heart.

WEDNESDAY

THOUGHTS FOR TODAY

Peace is, indeed, a very high value to God. There is a very clear command that tells us to "seek peace and pursue it" (1 Peter 3:11). We are not just to look around and see if it is there, we are to chase it until we find it. Peace doesn't just get dumped into our souls. Pursuit of peace is a very active venture in our lives. As we listen to the voice of the Spirit within us, He will create a greater and greater desire for peace. We, then, take the necessary steps to begin to pursue it. The results of our pursuit are up to God.

Pursuing peace involves several steps. *First we are to grow in purity.* As we have already learned, sin will block the peace between us and God. If we want peace, keeping short accounts with God is a requirement. We must not be afraid to ask the Spirit to show us areas in our lives that need to be cleaned up. He will do so gently and we will experience cleansing and an overall sense of well-being that can only be called *shalom*.

Second, we must practice contentment. We are to remember that we are pilgrims just passing through this world of time, and that eternity is our true home and our final destination. When we begin to think that way, possessions and events in this life take on a heavenly perspective and the contentment that grows becomes our peace.

THURSDAY
THOUGHTS FOR TODAY

God has told us to live in unity with our brothers and sisters in Christ. When that unity is disrupted, we are to be peacemakers. So *the third step in pursuing peace is to be willing to initiate reconciliation with someone who is unhappy with us.* Maybe it wasn't our fault. Maybe they haven't acknowledged their wrong. Maybe we are afraid we will not get a good response. But, there are times when we have to *make* peace; it won't just happen on its own. Initiating reconciliation is a very difficult thing to do. Maybe that is why Jesus pronounced special blessings upon those who are peacemakers (Matthew 5:9)

What are those blessings? The first is *rest*. Peace gives rest for our souls, ability to sleep soundly, and relief from anxiety. The second blessing is *health*: physical, emotional, and spiritual. When we realize all the diseases that can result from unrest within us and from conflicts with other people, we know that God's peace will be health to our bodies and our souls. A third blessing is renewed *relationships* that are built on honesty, forgiveness, service, and humility.

What greater peace is there in this world than healthy relationships with one another and with God? A final note: If we are living lives of authentic peace, others will notice. After all, peace is what they want, too. When they ask to have what we have, we can introduce them to Jesus, the sole source of true peace.

FRIDAY
READING GOD'S MESSAGE

Mark 4:36-41

What problem did the disciples encounter as they were crossing the Sea of Galilee?

What was their reaction to this difficulty?

Of what did the disciples accuse Jesus?

Why was their accusation unfair?

After He calmed the storm, for what did Jesus rebuke the disciples?

How did the disciples look at Jesus differently after the seas were calmed?

How can turning your storm over to Jesus' control give you peace?

SATURDAY
FOR PERSONAL REFLECTION

Describe to Jesus what you are facing right now in your life.

Tell Him how you feel about the troubles you have.

Ask Him to remind you of times He has rescued you in the past.

Thank Him for His power, His love, and His intervention for you.

Wait for the Spirit to speak peace to your soul.

Carry that peace with you as you trust your heavenly Father to take care of the problems you have given over to Him.

SUNDAY
PRAYER

Dear Lord, help me to trust and not be afraid. Fear comes in and faith flies out the door taking peace with it. You have given us the power of choice; why do I so often choose fear instead of faith?

Thank You for the encouragement to start over and to remember to ask for Your help before making the choice. Remembering is so important. You remind us so often in Your Word to remember Your mighty acts, remember how You saved the day with Your power, remember Your love. And, Jesus, You told Your disciples and us to remember You in the bread and the wine, "Do this in remembrance of Me" (Luke 22:19b). What a wonderful gift to remember You through communion with your body, the church. This brings peace through You, the Prince of Peace. We adore You, our Prince of Peace. Amen.

(18) Lois Tverberg, *Listening to the Language of the Bible* (Holland, Michigan: En-Gedi Resource Center), p. 13.

WEEK THIRTY-NINE

The Progress of Patience

"One moment of patience may ward off great disaster. One moment of impatience may ruin a whole life." – Chinese proverb

MONDAY
                THOUGHTS FOR TODAY

    Anger kills. Little by little, the annoyances, frustrations, and irritations that we feel begin to poison us and erode away at our health, our emotional stability, and our connection to God. Our natural response to the frustrations of life is some form of anger, not wild-eyed rage perhaps, but the kind of anger that leaves us uneasy and unsatisfied with our circumstances. The antidote to the poison of anger is patience.

    One of the characteristics of biblical patience has to do with *endurance or perseverance*. What kinds of things are we called upon to persevere through in this life? Sometimes we have to endure mistreatment – the kind of behaviors for which the natural reaction is striking out or hurting back. As God's children, enduring mistreatment means that . . .

> . . .we stop short of vengeance and, instead, allow God to bring justice in his own time. Patience does not allow us to repay hurt with hurt.

> . . . we trust in God's faithfulness. He will not abandon us when we are treated unfairly. He sees everything happening to us, but has a bigger picture than we know now. Someday our case will be heard in the courts of heaven and justice will prevail.

> . . . we pray for our tormentors. Jesus instructed us to pray for those who mistreat us. This is hard to do, but obedience will bring blessing to us and will keep our connection to God open and effective.

. . . we forgive those who hurt us. Jesus forgave those who were nailing Him to the cross. We are told to follow His example and forgive those who don't deserve our forgiveness so we can be healed of the pain we did not deserve to endure.

We love our comforts and sometimes expect that everything will fall into place for us if we just pray or go to church or read our Bibles. It doesn't work that way. There are many situations in each of our lives that we simply must accept and endure. In doing so, we find that we grow in strength. We understand others better. We can empathize with those who are in similar circumstances. Before we even realize it, we find that patience is raising its beautiful calm in our hearts. It is there, it is growing, and we are less angry. When patience appears, we have evidence that God is at work within us.

TUESDAY

MEDITATION

"So then, those who suffer according to God's will should commit themselves to their faithful Creator and continue to do good." (1 Peter 4:19)

Read through this verse a few times. Then allow the Spirit to highlight a word or phrase for a meditative focus. Write down any thoughts that come to your mind after your time of meditation.

WEDNESDAY

THOUGHTS FOR TODAY

Patience is a characteristic that we develop only over a long period of time. We cannot get it instantly. By definition, patience is tested only in times of trouble. So we don't really know how patient we are until we are called upon to endure problems or to deal with people who don't really deserve our gentle response. Once we are put in a position of having to exercise patience, how can we encourage its strength?

Patience grows when we reflect on God's patience toward us. We are told that God is slow to anger, He is gracious and longsuffering. When the understanding of how patient God is with us, we are more able to give away that patience to others. Reflecting on God's patience might require that we memorize a few Bible verses related to God's treatment of us. That way, when we are tempted to be impatient with others, we can recall those passages and allow the Spirit to let patience take over.

If we choose always to be confrontational or angry, the person who offends us tends to get defensive and rooted in continuing the same behavior. If we extend patience and grace, the possibility of change is alive and well.

We will not be perfect in exercising patience, so when we fail, we have to be patient with ourselves, too. We apologize if anger flares, we go to God when we cry out against having to endure, and we keep trying. Patience grows stronger with practice.

THURSDAY
THOUGHTS FOR TODAY

There are a number of things we can do to cultivate a more patient lifestyle. *First we can slow down.* Patience and hurry are incompatible. When we hurry, we are thinking only of ourselves and our own agendas and little room is left to extend the grace of patience to those around us.

Second, we can adopt God's view of others. "The Lord does not look at the things man looks at. Man looks at the outward appearance, but the Lord looks at the heart" (1 Samuel 16:7). When is the last time we have looked at a person's heart? When we try to understand what drives someone to act the way they do, we sometimes are able to see them as God does and then can respond with more compassion and patience.

Third, we should pray for wisdom. As we pray, we examine our own motives and thought patterns and, in doing so, open ourselves up the work of the Spirit within us.

Fourth, we must allow time for change. Patience cannot be imposed from the outside, it must come from within. Only God can do that kind of work and it may take a bit of time.

Finally, we need to learn to rely more on God to meet our needs than on other human beings. ". . . turn from expecting love, acceptance, and kindness from the world and fall more deeply in love with God" (19). The more we love our God, the more patient we will be. Guaranteed.

FRIDAY
READING GOD'S MESSAGE

Psalm 103

Write in your own words what this passage tells you about the patience of God.

Memorize verse 8 so you can recall it to your mind when you need to exercise patience with others. Write it here.

Think of instances in the life of Jesus when He showed patience to those around Him.

SATURDAY
FOR PERSONAL REFLECTION

Make a list of the things that you find yourself getting impatient about.

Ask God for wisdom in knowing how to handle each of these situations or individuals.

Listen for any direction that He gives. Write it down.

Check yourself in 30 days (mark it on your calendar) to see if you sense spiritual growth in your progress toward a more patient life.

SUNDAY
PRAYER

Lord, You show us in Your Word that patience and being slow to anger go together. You also say to be angry, but not to sin. You know, Father, that I can't even handle my own anger let alone other people's anger. I must give You my anger immediately for You to handle, because I can't. In exchange, You will give me patience and an understanding heart. You know me so well. I like that. You call me friend; You know me and still love me and want to spend time with me. How amazing is that? What a purpose in life---to get to know and have for a friend the Creator of the universe. I'm coming, Lord. In Your name, I'm coming. Amen.

(19) Gary Thomas, *The Glorious Pursuit* (Colorado Springs: NavPress, 1998), p. 126.

WEEK FORTY

Becoming Good

"A baptism of holiness, a demonstration of godly living is the crying need of our day." – C. S. Lewis

MONDAY
          THOUGHTS FOR TODAY

Every now and then on the radio I will hear recorded interviews of people who have been stopped on the street and asked a thought-provoking question. A recent one was "How would you answer if God said to you, 'Why should I let you into My heaven?'" Most of the answers began with a recounting of good deeds, sacrifices they have made for others, or the fact that they are better than most of the people around them.

According to the Bible, these are all wrong answers. But it is the trap of every religion or belief system in the world other than Christianity that, somehow. we can do something to earn God's favor. We cannot! The Bible is very clear on that matter. When we are dead in sins, there is nothing good living in us.

Nor do we need to become models of good behavior and then add Christ. We enter into a relationship with Jesus first, acknowledging our helplessness to be good at all. We come humbly and even desperately. We bring nothing to the table, but we simply accept, in faith, what He offers because we know that He means it when He says, *"Are you tired? Worn out? Burned out on religion? Come to me. Get away with me and you'll recover your life. I'll show you how to take a real rest. Walk with me and work with me—watch how I do it. Learn the unforced rhythms of grace. I won't lay anything heavy or ill-fitting on you. Keep company with me and you'll learn to live freely and lightly." (Matthew 11:28-30, The Message)*

Trying to be good on our own steam will simply wear us out, but when we are in the yoke with Jesus, we can rest from all our empty religion, all our futile attempts at being good. When we turn to Jesus as our only hope, goodness with follow as the Holy Spirit begins to work in us and to enable us to make decisions that honor our Savior.

A *desire* to be truly good, moral, upright people is born within us the moment we become a disciple of Jesus. If we don't have that desire, we need revisit our initial commitment to ensure that we are truly His followers. I imagine, though, that if you have come this far in our study, you are committed to growing in goodness. With that in mind, let's proceed.

What do you think of when you think of a good person? Usually things like integrity, generosity, honesty, trustworthiness, come to mind. Those are the kinds of characteristics that Paul meant when he wrote about the goodness that would come about in us as the Holy Spirit works in our lives (Galatians 5:22). In centuries past, we might have used the word *virtuous* to describe a good man or woman. Beginning with that understanding, we will unpack the concept of biblical goodness throughout this week.

TUESDAY

MEDITATON

"You are good, and what you do is good; teach me your decrees." (Psalm 119:68)

Allow the Spirit to reveal to your heart the truth of these words as you think about the goodness of God – both in what He is and in what He does. Write down any thoughts that you may have as you meditate in quietness.

WEDNESDAY

THOUGHTS FOR TODAY

Commentators have described biblical goodness as "moral energy". God will give us the energy we need to do the morally good and right thing, even when it's hard. And when we do the right thing because it is the right thing, we are living a life of moral excellence that honors God. At the same time, we are showing the world that we are following a higher authority than the culture around us. In fact, we are listening to the voice within us who calls us to live for Him, to be "royal" and "regal" in our moral and ethical decisions.

After all, we are children of the King!

How might our lives look if we are growing in goodness, living lives of moral excellence? It means

- telling the truth when it seems that a little white lie wouldn't hurt.

- resisting the temptation to cheat on a test when the grade is vitally important to passing the course.

- sharing some of our well-guarded cash with a friend who is in the middle of a financial struggle.

- taking responsibility for the snafu at work even though we could get by with letting someone else get blamed.

- having the baby even if it seems that having an abortion would make life easier for everyone, especially you.

- turning your back on the enticing relationship with a co-worker who is tempting you to be unfaithful to your spouse.

You get the idea. Moral excellence, virtue, goodness. Doing the right thing at the right time in the right way, Just as Jesus did.

THURSDAY

THOUGHTS FOR TODAY

There is a clear warning sign that we are being drawn away from growing in goodness: It is when we tend to compare ourselves to other people. We might find ourselves saying (or at least thinking) things like these:

- "I may not be perfect, but I'm not as bad as . . .."

- "I do tell little white lies occasionally, but you can't believe a word my brother-in-law says – and he claims to be a Christian, too"

- "Sure, I cheat on my income taxes, but doesn't everybody?"

There is only one standard – God's. None of us meets it, but as Christians, we will be showing a greater and greater goodness as we grow up spiritually

If, as followers of Christ, we are not demonstrating basic characteristics that even the world defines as good and moral, we will most certainly not be able to move forward in building a love relationship with Jesus. Goodness, a/k/a moral living or good character, is part of the very foundation of our lives. It is the minimum that is expected of a Christian.

If examination of our lives and our thoughts reveals that we are caught in a moral or ethical struggle, our only recourse it to turn to God and to commit ourselves to following His way no matter what. When we do that, He gives divine power (really, you can count on it) to enable us to make the next right moral decision, then the next, and the next until we find we are becoming people characterized by goodness.

FRIDAY
READING GOD'S MESSAGE

2 Peter 1:3-11

Read this passage carefully, then keep your Bible open as you answer these questions:

Why do you think Peter says that we should make every effort to add goodness to our faith? Why not just try to be good?

Based on our readings this week, what kind of efforts will most likely result in more moral and ethical living?

As we grow in goodness, what is the next characteristic we should add? And which ones after that?

In verse 8, what is the reason Peter gives for growing in all of these spiritual characteristics?

If we don't grow in these areas, what does this passage say we have forgotten? (v.9). Why is it important to remember where we have come from spiritually?

What two promises are given in verses 10 and 11?

SATURDAY
FOR PERSONAL REFLECTION

Take some time alone with God to examine your own heart and life practices. Make notes in your journal as you go through this exercise.

Step One: How do you think you are doing in developing the characteristic of goodness? Remember, don't compare yourself to anyone but Jesus.

Step Two: Ask the Holy Spirit to direct His light in the following areas:

- Any habit you should give up
- Any relationship that is dangerous for you
- Any temptation you are facing and need to address
- Any sin you need to confess
- Any people you may need to make amends with as a result of less-than-virtuous decisions you have made either recently or in the past

Step Three: If He brings any response to mind, respond in obedience and take the next right step toward living a life of goodness as Jesus did.

SUNDAY
PRAYER

Lord Jesus, I want Your life living in me, only then will doing good come from the right source. Please don't let me go in my own strength or my own desires. Help me to remember to heed Your invitation to come to You when am heavy-laden. You are calling me to spend time with You, and You will show me the path of life that is uniquely planned for me. Bless the Lord, O my soul. Amen.

WEEK FORTY-ONE

The Kindness of Caring

"Nothing can make our lives, or the lives of other people, more beautiful than perpetual kindness." – Leo Tolstoy

MONDAY
THOUGHTS FOR TODAY

Remember the craze that was going around a few years ago called "Random Acts of Kindness"? In that time, people were trying to figure out ways they could show kindness to others without being identified as the one who "committed" the good deed. Let's explore a couple of biblical concepts at work in the Random Acts of Kindness idea.

There are really three parts to authentic kindness. The first is a desire for the well-being of others. If we don't care, we don't act. Second is a sensitivity to the needs of other people. If we don't see, we don't respond. But, once we care and see, we want to do something about the situation. So, the third aspect of kindness is the thoughtful action that we take to meet the needs we see.

That's why the Random Acts of Kindness concept works so well. Thinking about ways to be kind to others increases our sensitivity to their needs and we begin to see ways we can help that we would not have seen otherwise. Too often, we look at people without seeing the pain, loneliness, sorrow, or unfulfilled desires of their hearts. A person filled with the kindness of the Spirit will have his/her eyes open to those needs and then, to the extent possible, do something about them.

One thing that motivates us, as Christians, to be kind to others is that God has been kind to us. We are told that one of the reasons Jesus came was to show us the kindness of God. (Ephesians 2:7 and Titus 3:4-5). How was Jesus kind? He healed, He fed, He listened, He taught, and He cared for those around him. Even the forceful confrontations with the religious leaders of the day were a kindness because, in revealing the truth about these leaders, Jesus was defending the weak who were being misused by them.

We are also told that it is the kindness of God that leads us to repent of our sinful lives and turn to Him in the first place. In *The Message,* it reads this way, "In kindness he takes us firmly by the hand and leads us into a radical life change" (Romans 2:4b). God shows us that kindness can confront and it can be firm, but it is always loving and always for the other person's best good. As God followers, we have every reason to be the kindest people on earth – always trying to find ways to do something good for those who need it.

TUESDAY

MEDITATION

"So, chosen by God for this new life of love, dress in the wardrobe God picked out for you: compassion, kindness, humility, quiet strength, discipline." (Colossians 3:12 *The Message*)

Meditate on these words, allowing God to show you how your life might be different if you were dressed in these Spirit-given characteristics. Make a note of anything you learn or understand at the end of your meditation time.

WEDNESDAY

THOUGHTS FOR TODAY

The Bible specifically tells us to be kind to the poor, strangers, widows, fatherless, neighbors, the burdened, the weak, enemies, and animals. If we think about it, we realize that at some time or another in our lives we fit into one or more of these categories (hopefully not animals!). We ourselves have felt alone or abandoned, we had a financial need, or we were weak or overburdened with circumstances of our lives. Because of this, we can empathize with those who suffer and, in doing so, can find a meaningful way to show kindness.

One way to be kind is by giving something material or monetary. God uses our attachment to possessions and money to test our faithfulness as His servants. We need to hold lightly to the things we own so we can freely give them to those in need. Earlier in my life, I found myself facing severe financial struggles for a few years. One Sunday as I was leaving church, our pastor's wife, aware of our needs, handed me an envelope. In it was a loving note and a check for $100. That money bought badly needed eyeglasses for my daughter but, more than that, brought unbelievable encouragement to my soul.

Someone noticed, cared, and acted. Now that my circumstances are better, I have found ways to give that $100 away over and over again. This dear lady's kindness has stretched to many others over the past thirty years and she doesn't even know it!

THURSDAY

THOUGHTS FOR TODAY

Another way to be kind is in our words. I taught high school with a woman who was a great example to me in this area. Every time a new classroom full of students came in, she surveyed the faces of all twenty-five or thirty of them until her eyes fell on one who seemed to need a gentle word. Then, as the class filed out at the end of the teaching hour, she made it a point to come face to face with that student and say something kind. It might be a compliment on his/her appearance, a recent achievement, a good attitude, or improved work. She felt that she had not fulfilled her teaching responsibilities for that hour until she had delivered a message of kindness to one who needed it most. By the end of every day, she had touched at least five lives with specifically directed words of encouragement and hope. I have often wondered how those kindnesses may have affected some of those students forever.

Kindness can be lived out in other ways as well. Did you ever think about the fact that being polite is really just a way of showing kindness? Forgiveness is another way. (Ephesians 4:32). What kinder thing can we do for someone than to be willing to restore our relationship with them?

So, let's get on with it and show kindness to someone today. As Ralph Waldo Emerson said, "You cannot do a kindness too soon, for you never know how soon it will be too late."

FRIDAY

READING GOD'S MESSAGE

2 Samuel 9:1-13

Jonathan, David's best friend, was killed in battle. To whom does David now want to show kindness?

Who seems to be directing David's act of kindness? (v. 3)

What special needs did Jonathan's son, Mephibosheth, have? (v. 3)

What kind things did David do for Mephibosheth?

What do these actions show us about the character of David?

How does this story motivate you to be kinder to others around you?

SATURDAY
FOR PERSONAL REFLECTION

Have you ever experienced someone else's kindness? Think back on the situation and how their actions or words made you feel.

Has God put you through experiences that make you want to treat others more kindly? What are they?

Is there someone in your life right now to whom you can show a special kindness?

Pray, asking God to open your eyes to needs around you and then go out and commit kindness whenever possible.

SUNDAY
PRAYER

Lord, You have shown me that kindness is not natural to me. I had to ask specifically for that fruit of the Spirit and then wait for it to manifest. One day You whispered to me that I had done a kind act. I knew You were right and I was so pleased, but I couldn't remember what it was. You whispered again that not remembering a kind act is part of kindness. I loved that teaching, Lord. As I grow in kindness, You will teach me other things about it. You make learning such fun and so exciting. Nothing excites more than a transformed life---mine! Thank You, Jesus, for giving me these chances to be like You in Your world. Amen.

WEEK FORTY-TWO

Under Control

"We seek satisfaction of our spiritual longing in a host of ways that may have very little to do with God." – Gerald May

MONDAY

THOUGHTS FOR TODAY

We are invited on every front to be self-indulgent. Advertising tells us there are things and products we didn't even know about that, now that we know, we simply cannot live without. Psychologists tell us to identify and follow our desires. Not all new products are bad and it is sometimes right to follow our hearts, but the overriding message seems to be "if it feels good, do it." That philosophy runs counter to the message given in the Bible.

We need self-control and are the benefactors when we choose to develop this spiritual characteristic in our lives. The Greek word translated *self-control* in the Bible actually means *inner strength*. Who among us would not want to have inner strength?

- Strength to enable us to make right decisions even when driven by the world around us to go with the flow.

- Strength to enable us to keep our bodies in good condition so that we are able to enjoy physical activities and have stamina to work hard and long.

- Strength to be healthy emotionally so we can enter into loving and nurturing relationships with others.

When we see these benefits, maybe we can agree that self-control is not bad after all!

The obstacle for many of us, though, is that the inner strength we want is not instantaneously given. It is developed over many months and years of exercising the muscle of self-control on multiple fronts. We need to control our *bodies* in areas of food and drink, work ethic, and sexuality. We need to control our *emotions* by dealing biblically with anger, bitterness, and self-pity. We need to control our *minds* by guarding what enters them and focusing our thoughts on things that are pleasing to God. Self-control in all of these areas is a difficult assignment, and even the saintly apostle Paul admitted to sometimes being defeated in areas of self-control. If it were easy, we all would be models of perfection. It is not easy, but it *is* very important.

Self-control is an important muscle to strengthen primarily because of the spiritual war in which we are engaged. The Bible tells us that sinful desires within us actually war against our souls (1 Peter 2:11). We are also told that there are two natures within us, one warring against the other. The only way to win a war of the inward spirits is to allow a spiritual self-control to govern – a self-control that is supernaturally given when we give up ourselves to the Holy Spirit's control.

TUESDAY
MEDITATION

". . . put off your old self, which is being corrupted by its deceitful desires; to be made new in the attitude of your minds. . ." (Ephesians 4:22-23)

Think about these words and how a new attitude might strengthen your self-control. Allow the Spirit to make these words real to your heart. Write down any insights you may have.

WEDNESDAY
THOUGHTS FOR TODAY

There are steps we can take to begin to exercise our self-control muscle. First we need to know the standards revealed in the Bible. We don't know what we should be striving for until we know what God says. His tells us everything we need to know about the behavior He expects from us. So, the *first step* toward self-control is to dig into the Bible and get our direction from its message.

The *second step* is to do a self-assessment. In what areas of self-control do we most often fail? With the Spirit's help, we can think of ways we can overcome our weaknesses in those areas.

As a *third step*, we can try a holy experiment by committing to giving up temporary pleasures in order to please God. We can tell God we are more interested in pleasing Him that in being gratified physically or emotionally. Then we can try a time of fasting from food, sweets, television, or some other activity that we are willing to give up as a spiritual work-out in order to develop self-control.

When we do this, we are letting God and ourselves know that we are serious about emphasizing the spiritual over the physical, the eternal over the temporary, and God over self. Then we can take joy in the spiritual pleasures that will come as a result of our commitment. When the spiritual pleasures become a greater draw to us than physical pleasures, we will have learned the discipline of self-control.

THURSDAY
THOUGHTS FOR TODAY

A *fourth step* in developing self-control is mind-control. Spiritual battles are won or lost in the mind. We must learn to put a wall of protection around our brains and carefully guard the gate, allowing only the things that contribute to our physical, spiritual, or emotional health to enter. We must develop an awareness of our thoughts, discarding those that are negative, lustful, self-indulgent, or self-pitying and instead, filling our minds with memorized scripture and continual praise of our father in heaven. If we can keep our brains chock full of the good and true, there will be no room for that which would mislead us into thinking that self-indulgence is good for us.

Fifth, if we are serious about self-control, we should find a friend who knows God's standards and loves us enough to hold us accountable for the discipline goals we have set. We are many more times stronger with someone than we are alone. Many times we are able to overcome small issues of self-control with just the Spirit's help, but the major areas of struggle in our life can often be overcome only through the help of others of like mind. God intends for us to help and support each other in this journey.

Last, we must continually pray for strength to make good choices. The Holy Spirit is our greatest ally in the development of self-control. He is our workout partner and will supernaturally increase the results of our own efforts if we allow Him to.

FRIDAY
READING GOD'S MESSAGE

1 Peter 1:13-21

What commands are given in these verses?

What roles do the mind, emotions, and will play in being obedient to these commands?

Why does it take self control in order to be holy as we are told to do in verse 16?

Why do we have hope in being able to live disciplined lives? (vv. 17-21).

Thank God for the power He gives you to live the life He envisions for you.

SATURDAY
FOR PERSONAL REFLECTION

Spend some time in prayer asking the Spirit to reveal to you areas in your life in which you need to practice better self-control.

Speech?	Healthy living?
Food?	Time use?
Drink?	Attitudes?
Sexuality?	Anger?
Ambition?	Resentment?
Exercise?	Wayward thoughts?

As God reveals the areas He wants you to deal with, commit to Him that you will do what He says. Then outline in writing a first step you will take for developing self-control in any areas He reveals.

SUNDAY

PRAYER

Lord, it is so true that without You I can do nothing; grant me Your grace just for today to start partnering with You in every area of my life. I submit every area to You and together we can start fresh today. You will show me the way and I promise to follow. The old is passing away and You are making all things new. New is good and fresh and exciting. I'll never be done being new. Thank You for this eternal purpose that You have given me. Glory be to You, O Lord.

WEEK FORTY-THREE

The Joy of Gentleness

"Nothing is so strong as gentleness, nothing so gentle as real strength." – Francis de Sales

MONDAY

THOUGHTS FOR TODAY

Probably there is no better picture of gentleness than that of a mother holding her newborn child. Her movements are slow, her voice is quiet, her touch is soft. Now, imagine that the father of that baby is a hefty professional football player. He is rough and tough and used to tossing footballs into the air and opposing players to the ground. Picture him as he takes his newborn son for the first time. This strong giant of a man tenderly strokes the baby's head and coos soothing sounds into his ear. As we watch, we realize that we are witnessing gentleness with a capital "G". The stronger a person is, the more important it is for him to be gentle with those who are weak.

We sometimes think of gentleness as being borne of weakness. That is not true. If we look at these two parents, we see that the stronger the person, the greater need there is for showing gentleness. Jesus embodied the limitless power of God. Yet, there was no one gentler in dealing with those who were weak than He was. As we grow stronger spiritually, we are more and more capable of being gentle to those around us.

There is sometimes confusion between gentleness and meekness. Gentleness is active – it is the part of the definition of how we should treat others. Meekness is more passive and describes how we are to react when others mistreat us. Both characteristics are exhibited in our lives only when we are strong. They are the ultimate examples of power under control.

Gentleness might be seen as exercising self-control for the benefit of others. Other characteristics related to gentleness might include consideration, sensitivity, respect, understanding, generosity, fairness, mercy, reasonability, tenderness, and caring. Gentleness is not severe, does not rigidly follow rules, and is not harsh. As author

Jerry Bridges said, "The human personality is fragile; handle with care." (20). Gentleness does just that.

    The one to whom we look for the grace of gentleness is God himself. Psalm 18:35 says, "Thy gentleness makes me great" (NASB). Paul refers in Corinthians to the gentleness of Christ. The prophet Zechariah tells of the king coming gently and on a donkey. Jesus showed humility and grace instead of arrogance and terror. He showed us what gentleness could be. Now, let's close our eyes and visualize how we would look, move, and sound if we were gentler people. If gentleness were to grow in our hearts, how would we change? Would people react to us differently if we were gentler?

TUESDAY

MEDITATION

"Let your gentleness be evident to all. The Lord is near." (Philippians 4:5)

Think about this instruction and allow the Spirit to show you how gentleness can better be evidenced in your life. Write down anything that He brings to your mind.

WEDNESDAY

THOUGHTS FOR TODAY

    There are several biblical directives related to gentleness and each of them reveals something different about this characteristic The first is the command in Philippians that was the focus of our meditation yesterday. We learn from this verse that if we have the trait of gentleness, others will see it. The next command is in Colossians where we are told to put on gentleness as if we were putting on a piece of clothing. In other words, gentleness is a choice. We choose to put it on daily. When we get dressed in the morning, we are to make sure one of the items we put on is gentleness. The third command is in 1 Timothy where we are told to pursue gentleness. Gentleness is elusive, it escapes us, and we have to chase it. God wants us to be serious about gentleness!

    Maybe the first step in pursuing gentleness is to take a

gentleness inventory. Let's ask ourselves these questions:

> Do people feel at ease in my presence? If not, why not?
> Do they feel guilty when they are around me?
> Are people able to be honest with me?
> Is anyone afraid of me?
> Is my voice harsh or loud?
> Are people comfortable visiting in my home?
> Do others perceive me as understanding and empathetic?
> Do my hands convey love?

The answers to these questions might help us to see the areas of gentleness that we need to pursue. Becoming gentle is a process. We are now simply identifying the starting point.

THURSDAY
THOUGHTS FOR TODAY

How do we begin to cultivate this gentleness in our hearts? First, we have to *understand human frailty*. The people around us are not perfect, but they need our gentleness. The more we can empathize with them, see their point of view, and feel their pain, the more we will find the spirit of gentleness welling up within us and our interactions with them will heal instead of hurt.

We are to determine that we will, in all circumstances, *exercise gentleness*. This requires that we slow down, confront in love when confrontation is necessary, and lead without coercion or manipulation. But, in every case, we make gentleness the ruling factor in our conversations and in the decisions we make knowing that our decisions affect others.

As we *meditate on Scriptures* related to gentleness, we open the way for God to show us what a gentle life is like. As we submit to the truth of the Word of God, it begins to become part of the fabric of our lives and gentleness will be one of the strongest threads.

Along with Scripture meditation, we will want to *pray for growth in gentleness*. If we ask the Spirit to convict us of times of ungentle behavior and attitudes, He will empower us to develop this very powerful characteristic. At some point we will realize that changes have occurred and we will be able to claim the description in 1 Peter 3:4 of the "unfading beauty of a gentle and quiet spirit."

FRIDAY
READING GOD'S MESSAGE

Isaiah 40:10-11

What does this passage tell us about the power of God?

What does it tell us about His gentleness?

How are these characteristics of God different than what we often see in powerful people?

What are your feelings as you read about God's power and His gentleness?

SATURDAY
FOR PERSONAL REFLECTION

List some ways in which God has gently cared for you through your life. Thank Him.

Ask Him to show you ways to become gentler and more loving toward those around you.

Ask Him to show you anything in your life that needs to be changed in order to allow the Spirit to work with you in developing a gentle spirit.

Write down any insights or instructions that you are given.

SUNDAY
PRAYER

Father, Your gentleness has drawn me to You; You are a gentle

Abba and You show Your love in always being there for me no matter how selfish or undesirable I may be. This is very humbling. The Creator of the world wants to spend time with me. Teach me Your ways, O Lord, and I will allow Your grace to keep me teachable. In Your name I pray. Amen.

(20) Jerry Bridges, *The Practice of Godliness* (Colorado Springs, NavPress, 1983, 1996), p. 181.

WEEK FORTY-FOUR

Sticking With It

"A true friend advises justly, assists readily, adventures boldly, takes all patiently, defends courageously, and continues a friend unchangeably." – William Penn

MONDAY

THOUGHTS FOR TODAY

Have you ever had a faithful friend? One who could be counted on even if you called at 4 a.m.? We all need at least one friend like that: A confidante who is dependable, trustworthy, reliable, honest, and loyal. We all need to *be* a friend like that to someone else, too. As we delve into the concept of being faithful, we find that faithfulness to God and faithfulness to other human beings go hand-in-hand.

Business leaders say that success in any field is not so much dependent upon the big decisions that are made once in a while as it is upon doing the same right little things over and over again. Those kinds of things include being on time, planning the work day the evening before, returning all calls within a 24-hour period, treating people as valued team members, and not procrastinating. Researchers have concluded that business success is more dependent upon consistency and faithfulness than it is upon inspired ideas or lucky breaks.

The same principle holds true in our relationships. A good marriage or a long-term friendship is more dependent upon the day-to-day give and take of talking to one another and maneuvering through the daily grind than it is upon the great romantic dinners, vacations together, support during a crisis, or even significant milestones. To us as humans, little things mean a lot – the "How are you?" phone calls, the smile when we walk in the door, the pat on the back, and the sense of being loved and accepted. Relationships last because our characters and the characters of those we relate to prove to be consistent and dependable.

The principle of faithfulness is no less vital in our spiritual development. It's the little things we do over and over again that continue to take us into the presence of God, enable us to receive His direction, and encourage us to submit to His authority in our lives. Those things include daily Bible reading and prayer as well as practicing other disciplines such as meditation, scripture memorization, church attendance, and engaging in personal times of worship.

None of these requires great sacrifice on our part. None requires us to retreat to the desert and leave all earthly comforts. None requires huge blocks of time. But with God, too, the little things mean a lot. Faithfulness may begin with our commitment to these small things, but as the faithfulness factor grows in our lives, we begin to see results. Our consistency will be rewarded with answered prayers, fulfilling relationships, and blessings greater than we can imagine.

TUESDAY

MEDITATION

"Now it is required that those who have been given a trust must prove faithful." (1 Corinthians 4:2)

Meditate on this verse and ask the Spirit to reveal to you His message for you today. Write down whatever comes to your mind.

WEDNESDAY

THOUGHTS FOR TODAY

The first part to learning faithfulness is *turning our back on self-centered living.* If we can get ourselves out of the focus and turn, instead, to others, we will find it is easier to be faithful.

- Instead of wondering if our own needs are met, we will look toward meeting the needs of others.

- Instead of quitting a friendship if our feelings get hurt, we will hang in there and work out the problems.

- Instead of bailing out when the going gets rough, we will be able to be committed to a higher value than our own happiness.

Re-focusing our attention on others requires that we respect them in spite of their failings, love them even when they are not acting lovably, and serve them when they don't deserve it*. As we do these things dependably and consistently, we will grow in faithfulness. We will set our course for God's glory and refuse to give up.

The second part of faithfulness has to do with *adopting a pattern of God-centered living.* We do this by understanding the faithfulness of God. His character will grow within us as we set it before us through prayer, meditation, and study. As we do this, we will also learn that we can trust God to help us be faithful. Sometimes it seems impossible to hang in there with someone who doesn't deserve our loyalty. But the impossible becomes possible when God is in it. And faithfulness is His plan.

*Please note that unthinking faithfulness to an abusive person is not required. In such cases, wise counsel should be sought and decisions made accordingly. Faithfulness to God is what counts in these situations.

THURSDAY
THOUGHTS FOR TODAY

One of the most reassuring things we can count on in our lives is God's faithfulness to us. Here are a few scriptures that tell us God is . . .

faithful to all his promises.	Psalm 145:13
faithful to keep us strong.	1 Corinthians 1:8-9
faithful when we are tempted.	1 Corinthians 10:13
faithful to forgive us.	1 John 1:9
faithful when we suffer.	1 Peter 4:19

We can count on God to do whatever He has said He would do, to support us when we are weak, to forgive us when we confess our failures, and to encourage us when we are going through difficult times.

What God is to us, we should be to others. Let's commit to looking around us and being aware when our unwavering support will be a lifesaver to someone else. Faithfulness is keeping on even when keeping on is not easy to do.

- It is walking through the hard times when it would be easier to quit.

- It is trusting God when He says He will not give us more than we can bear.

- It is following God's plan for our lives even when we think we have a better way.

- It is doing the right thing even if it is the hard thing, and keeping on doing it with our eye toward the goal of God's "Well done, good and faithful servant!" (Matthew 25:21).

FRIDAY
READING GOD'S MESSAGE

Matthew 25:14-30

Who do the master and servants represent in this story?

How did the master describe the first two servants?

How did he describe the third servant?

Why did the master take the one talent from the wicked servant?

What does this parable teach us about how important faithfulness is to God?

SATURDAY
FOR PERSONAL REFLECTION

In what relationship in your life to you need to be more dependable or consistent?

What can you begin to do today to begin to put faithfulness into practice in that relationship?

Evaluate your faithfulness to God. Could your relationship Him be strengthened by greater faithfulness in the little things such as Bible reading, prayer, meditation, worship, and so on? Which of these is the weakest link in your spiritual development?

Spend some time in prayer asking God to show you where you need to be more faithful to Him or to others. Then allow the Spirit to unfold ways in which you can be obedient in greater faithfulness day by day. Write down what you learn. Then put it into practice right away

SUNDAY
PRAYER

Holy Spirit, as I spend time with You, listening to You speak to my spirit, I will daily have the plan for my life. As I walk this out on a daily basis I will never doubt Your faithfulness to me. Thank You for Your ministry of conviction of sin to help me keep short accounts with You and stay in that state of forgiveness. This helps me to be compassionate and forgiving to those around me. Let this circle of love ever keep expanding. I ask all this in Your precious name, Jesus. Amen.

WEEK FORTY-FIVE

At Your Service

"We are, all of us, never-ceasing spiritual beings with a unique eternal calling to count for good in God's great universe." – Dallas Willard

MONDAY

THOUGHTS FOR TODAY

We have spent some time now growing in relationship with our Father in Heaven and, more recently, in allowing the Holy Spirit to change us to look more and more like Jesus. Now it gets even better: God has a plan for using us to bring honor to Him through a uniquely-defined role for service in His kingdom. We will talk about that over the next few weeks.

Serving others is not the top things on most people's priority lists. Our ideal life probably has a lot more to do with being served than in serving. Jesus turned the natural view upside down when He came to earth and told us that the person who was to be great in His kingdom was the one who serves. What does it take to have the heart of a servant?

First, we have to be willing to be humble. There are many jobs that confront us just in living our lives that are not pleasant. It takes a humble person to clean toilets, sweep sidewalks, and pick up garbage. But these are jobs that need to be done. The servant is the person who does not weigh the importance of the job, but the importance of meeting a need. My friend Jennifer has a really queasy stomach when it comes to cleaning up vomit. But human bodies sometimes upchuck and if there are little children in the home, the chances of the vomit actually hitting the toilet are slim. Jennifer says that she has never had to clean up vomit when her husband is home. He knows her aversion to the job and simply does it without complaint. With tears in her eyes, she goes on to say that when she sees Karl cleaning up after their children this way, she sees Jesus.

Now, realize that Karl is a professional, highly educated, acknowledged in his field, and admired by many. From the natural perspective, he is far too important to be on his knees cleaning up vomit. But Karl exemplifies the heart of humility as he lovingly serves his wife and children. His attitude of humble service brings the heart of Jesus into their home.

Second, we have to serve out of love. Someone has pointed out that the cross has two beams. The first points heavenward and connects us with God. The second points outward and connects us with each other. All of our service for our fellow-man comes out of the picture of the cross and the love that Jesus showed for us when He died there. Because He loved us, we love Him and, then, turn to love others. If we are not serving out of love, we will expect repayment or, at the very least, gratitude. When we serve others because we love, our service is effective to those we serve and fulfilling to us. No further reward is needed.

TUESDAY

MEDITATION

"So I will gladly spend for you everything I have and expend myself as well." (2 Corinthians 12:15a)

Meditate on these words of the apostle Paul to the believers in Corinth. Allow the Spirit to make real to you the attitude of heart necessary to be a servant as Paul was. Make some notes as you sit with this verse in God's presence.

WEDNESDAY

THOUGHTS FOR TODAY

Mother Theresa is quoted as saying, "We don't do great things. We do little things with great love." Anyone who has heard of Mother Theresa knows that she was a humble servant. No job was too demeaning including picking maggots off a person recently brought in from the streets. If it needed to be done, she was willing to do it. Love was the force that drove her to see the need and to respond willingly.

Only God can weigh the value of our service. We can work hard day and night to provide service, but if we are doing it for the paycheck, for the public recognition, or even for the gratitude of those we serve, our service doesn't count much in God's economy. But even the smallest service we give because we are loved and, thus, can love, will be used by God in ways that we cannot even envision. Love serves. Any motivation that is not as pure as love results in natural service. It takes God-given love to serve supernaturally.

Only God can make our service effective. We all know of massive efforts to help the needy that have failed miserably. Then we hear stories of small groups that are having phenomenal success in helping people get back on their feet financially, in walking successfully through release from addiction, and in healing broken relationships. Effectiveness of service goes far deeper than dollar amounts or numbers served. It has to do with eternally changed lives. If our service is God-directed and love-motivated, it will matter, for now and forever.

THURSDAY
THOUGHTS FOR TODAY

Paul stated, "...as we have opportunity, let us do good to all people, *especially to those who belong to the family of believers.*" (Galatians 6:10; emphasis added). As Christians, we have a responsibility to help the needy in our world, but we have an even greater responsibility to serve each another.

Scripture says that we are members of one body, the body of Christ, and, as such, each part of the body is designed to support and work with the other parts. Physically, if you cut your finger, the rest of your body knows it. White blood cells are sent to fight off infection, and the skin cells work furiously to begin to heal the wound. The analogy works in the body of Christ, too. If one member hurts, the rest need to rush healing and protection to that member until he is fully functioning once again.

Similarly, if we are lifting a heavy load, all the muscles of the physical body work together under the strain so the back, arms, or shoulders don't have to handle it alone. The same is true with members of our Christian body. If someone is struggling with a life burden too heavy to carry alone, we help him for as long as it takes. What one person cannot bear alone, many working together can bear without strain. In following this God-directed pattern, our service becomes support to those who are in need and, as a result, the entire body thrives.

FRIDAY
READING GOD'S MESSAGE

1 Corinthians 12:12-31

In what way is the church compared to a human body?

Why is it important that various members of the church have various functions just as various parts of the body have various functions?

What should our attitude be toward those whose abilities or roles are different than ours?

Write, in your own words, the messages given in verses 25 and 26.

How does this understanding affect your treatment of other members of the body of Christ?

SATURDAY
FOR PERSONAL REFLECTION

Is there someone whom you need to be serving?

Ask God to show you the most effective way to serve this person. Then serve, knowing that God will weigh your service based on the heart of humility and love with which the service is given.

Is there some area in which you need to be served?

If so, ask God for wisdom in knowing how to present your need to someone who can help. Then move forward as He directs.

SUNDAY
PRAYER

Lord, there have been times when I thought I knew better how to serve someone and did not ask You; forgive me for those presumptuous sins. You know all things, You know each person intimately and will give me that wisdom if I ask and wait on You to give the answer. Help me to walk in Your timing and to be cheerful about it. If the answer is delayed, give me the patience to wait for it. You have a purpose that I don't always understand. I submit to You, Lord, Holy Father, almighty God. In Jesus' name. Amen.

WEEK FORTY-SIX

Equipped to Serve

"Only when we're thoroughly convinced that the Christian life is entirely of grace are we able to serve God out of a grateful and loving heart." – Jerry Bridges

MONDAY

THOUGHTS FOR TODAY

God thinks of everything! Last week we talked about the fact that He wants us to serve each other. We are to help the needy, support the weak, and especially to take care of those who are members of the body of Christ as we are. We hear that command and we immediately get worried. What can we do? After all we have limited time, very little money, and not very much talent. How can we possibly serve?

God knew we would ask and He has an answer. He tells us not to worry because He will give us abilities and talents that we can use to carry out His plan. He calls these special abilities *spiritual gifts* because they are given by the Spirit. Spiritual gifts are like human talents on steroids and the steroid, in this case, is the Holy Spirit. When we put into practice the gifts that God gives, we are able to do things we could never even dream of on our own. When we are relying on the Spirit's gifts, we find that what we do and what we say has power and effectiveness that we don't have in any other way. We are supernaturally gifted to do supernatural work. If that is the case, we should take some time to find out more about this unique power source.

What are some of the gifts that the Spirit gives? We read lists in Romans 12:6-8, 1 Corinthians 12:8-10, Ephesians 4:11, and 1 Peter 4:10-11. We will look at them more specifically next week. But before we do that, we should know that there are some rules that govern these gifts.

First, the Spirit decides who gets what gift. It is a gift, after all and we don't shop for our own gifts. Whatever He gives us, we are to use. We are not to look at someone else and say or think, "If I just had that gift, I could do more for God." Also, *we should be*

aware that the gifts are given to be used for one purpose: building up the church (knowing that the Bible defines the church as all those who are followers of Christ).

For us, this means that we are to find what our gift is and then turn around and use it among fellow believers for the purpose of serving them and, thus, we will strengthen each other's faith, support each others' needs, and encourage each other to do good things, to know God better, and to spread the message of God's great love to those who may not yet have heard and understood it.

TUESDAY

MEDITATION

"God doesn't want us to be shy with His gifts, but bold and loving and sensible." (2 Timothy 1:7 *The Message*)

Quiet your mind and meditate on these words asking the Spirit to make them real to your heart. After a time of stillness before God, write down any thoughts that you have.

WEDNESDAY

THOUGHTS FOR TODAY

Here are examples of gifts of the Spirit as listed various passages in the Bible: prophecy, teaching, knowledge, evangelism, healing, wisdom, encouragement, faith, miracles, hospitality, apostleship, discernment, helps, serving, administration, tongues, mercy, and giving. While this list is interesting and important to know, there is nothing in the Bible indicating the lists of the Spirit gifts are exhaustive. Some passages allude to other gifts and those passages make us think that God gives gifts as He desires and is not subject to a specific, limiting list.

The lists are given as guides to help us understand ways in which God may choose to use us. But God will not force any gift upon us. We have to be willing to receive what He is offering to give. Once we are willing, then God knows that His gift will not sit unused, but will be put to work to strengthen his church.

- So, we express our willingness to be used.

- Then we ask God to begin to show us the way or ways in which He has gifted us for supernaturally empowered service within His kingdom.

- After that, as we found yesterday, our job is to be bold, loving, and sensible with whatever gift God has given us.

We don't have to conjure up abilities, persuasion, or programs in order to serve God effectively. *We simply have to be willing to use the gifts that the Spirit gives.* In God's world, willingness precedes usefulness.

THURSDAY
THOUGHTS FOR TODAY

Another thing to remember as we begin to look at our own gifts and how God wants us to use them, is that *we have been placed in a particular place, with certain people, at a specific time, for a sacred purpose.* Esther was a young Jewish woman, taken into the harem of a wicked Persian king and eventually made queen. When an evil plan was hatched to destroy all Jews in the Persian empire, Esther's uncle Mordecai heard of it and asked Esther to petition the king for the lives of her people. She hesitated because approaching the king without invitation was to risk being sentenced to death. But Mordecai intrigued Esther by wondering aloud if she might have been brought to her royal position for the very purpose of getting the king's attention so her people could survive. Thus emboldened (and after prayer and fasting), she entered the king's court, received his welcome, and pled her case. The Jewish people were saved from annihilation as a result of her using her abilities and position effectively on their behalf.

When we think about what we can do to serve God, we look upward to see what He desires in our lives, we look inward for the spiritual gifts that are available to be used in service, and we look around us at the needs and opportunities that are in our homes, our workplaces, our neighborhoods, our churches, and our culture. Then we go to work knowing God's power is working through us.

FRIDAY

READING GOD'S MESSAGE

Acts 16:6-15

How were Paul's plans changed by the leading of the Holy Spirit?

Who was affected in Philippi because Paul was obedient?

What spiritual gifts did Paul use in his ministry to Lydia?

What was the result of his being in the right place and using his Spirit-empowered gifts?

Pray, asking God to show you how you can affect those whom you meet today.

SATURDAY

FOR PERSONAL REFLECTION

Think of the people in your life who look to you with trust. Is there one (or more) who needs to experience God's love and truth through you?

Do you think you might have been placed in that person's life for that very purpose? Why or why not?

Is there any action you should take concerning this person (or persons)?

As you go through your routine today, ask God to reveal to you any people He is placing in your path so that you can serve them in some way with the spiritual gifts He has already provided you. Then go about your day in sharpened awareness of those around you who have needs and reach out to them in boldness and love if the Spirit directs.

SUNDAY

PRAYER

Lord, you have something for me to do and I covenant with You through Jesus' blood that I will be available for Your initiatives for me. Help me keep my eyes off other people and what they are doing or not doing and just pay attention to my directives. I hear You say, "Clear your schedule and be available to Me. I am the Master Scheduler." Yes, Lord, I agree; You are the Master Scheduler. In You there is fullness of joy. Blessed be the name of the Lord. Amen.

WEEK FORTY-SEVEN

Recognizing Our Gifts

"Desire that your life count for something great! Long for your life to have eternal significance. Want this! Don't coast through life without a passion." – John Piper

MONDAY

THOUGHTS FOR TODAY

Many people have said to me through the years, "I don't have any talents. I don't see how God can use me." That statement is absolutely contrary to the teaching of the Bible and I believe it breaks God's heart to hear us say it. God does not want us to be proud, but neither does He want us to think He cannot use us for His work. The great preacher D. L. Moody once said, "No one can sum up all God is able to accomplish through one solitary life, wholly yielded, adjusted, and obedient to Him." Wouldn't you or I like to be that totally committed man or woman? Our commitment plus God's power will yield unbelievable results.

We sometimes confuse human abilities with the spiritual giftedness. We may not feel very talented and, therefore, believe that we cannot serve God. God says, however, that when we are weak, then He can be strong. Maybe seeing our own weakness is the first step in recognizing our spiritual gifts! The main purpose in serving God is to allow Him to receive glory. If we are filled to overflowing with natural talent, we will most likely think we are able to accomplish great things for God on our own. Others, too, might look at our achievements and comment on how talented we are. But God has a different plan. He wants us to serve Him out of weakness so it will be very clear that the results of our service are because of Him and not because of us.

The Spirit has given each of us at least one special gift to be used in serving God. Our job is to identify what that gift is. Let's take a look at some the gifts identified in Scripture and begin to understand what they mean when applied to building up the church and bringing glory to God. Here are the first few:

Teaching: Those who love learning and devote time to studying the Bible are those who most likely have the gift of teaching. A teacher shares what he or she has learned in a way that helps the student have a truer and deeper understanding of God.

Knowledge: This gift is closely related to teaching, but involves special understanding given by the Spirit as Scripture is read, studied, and meditated upon.

Encouragement: Some are specially enabled to come alongside another to build them up, to comfort them, to pick them up when they have fallen.

TUESDAY
MEDITATION

"Each one should use whatever gift he has received to serve others, faithfully administering God's grace in its various forms." (1 Peter 4:10)

Read this verse over several times and then allow the Spirit to show you a phrase on which to meditate until He makes the message real and meaningful to you. Take notes!

WEDNESDAY
THOUGHTS FOR TODAY

Here are other ways the Spirit uses us in the work of the church:

Prophecy: A prophet speaks the truth. Today, the role of a prophet is usually practiced through preaching. A person preaching is taking God's message (found in Scripture and through the Holy Spirit) and delivering it to those who listen. A prophet, in this sense, speaks for God to the people.

Faith: A person of faith lives with well-founded optimism, always seeing what God can do even in seemingly hopeless situations.

Wisdom: This gift evidences itself by a depth of practical, enlightened understanding which is based upon both experience and Scripture.

Discernment: The person with this gift knows when someone is being deceitful and is enabled by God to share that understanding and protect God's family from being misled.

Helping: Those with this gift are specially enabled to see another's needs and to assist in meeting those needs in the most practical and effective ways possible.

Serving: A person with the gift of serving will provide special and personal service to another person or persons delivering it with great love and humility.

Administration: This gift is used for decision-making and guidance in overseeing the direction and oversight of a church.

Ruling: This gift is exercised by those who direct specific programs, projects, and activities of a church.

Mercy: The person with this gift shows compassion for those in need, whether than need is spiritual or physical.

Giving: The gift of giving is evidenced by one who shares freely whatever he/she has, usually money or possessions.

THURSDAY
THOUGHTS FOR TODAY

How can we know which of these gifts are ours? *First, we ask the Holy Spirit to show us* by highlighting a particular gift as we pray and as we observe needs among the believers with whom we worship and serve.

Second, we try serving in areas of interest or toward which we sense a tug. If that service results in good response from those with whom we work and if there is an echoing approval from the Spirit within us, we can move forward expanding our use of that gift to the glory of God.

I have the gift of teaching. I know partly because I love to study and learn about God. Then when I consciously made myself available to serve God, I sensed the Spirit directing me to begin teaching women. Within a few days of that direction, a spiritual friend called to ask if I would consider teaching a Saturday morning women's Bible study at her church. With the clear direction I had already received from the Spirit, I couldn't say no!

As soon as the group began to meet, I received feedback from the women about all they were learning and how the study we undertook together encouraged their spiritual growth. That was the confirmation I needed that the gift I sensed was, in truth, a specially empowered gift of the Spirit. There is great joy in finding and using the gifts we have been specifically given to serve God and each other. Have you found the way and the place where God is waiting to use you?

FRIDAY
READING GOD'S MESSAGE

Ephesians 4:1-16

What kind of attitude are we to have as we serve God? (vv.1-3)

What is Paul's special emphasis in verses 4-6?

What is the purpose of spiritual gifts according to verses 12 and 13?

According to verse 16, how is the body of Christ built up?

Pray a prayer of commitment telling God that you will do whatever it is He wants you to do within His church if He will simply reveal to you what it is and will open a door of opportunity so you can use the gift He has given.

SATURDAY
FOR PERSONAL REFLECTION

What are some specific talents that you have?

Is there an interest or ability you have that might give you insight in the spiritual gift God may have given you?

Talk to a trusted friend about what you perceive to be your spiritual gift and ask for confirmation or non-confirmation from him/her.

Put your gift to work by seeking opportunities to serve others. Ask God to reveal through feedback from those you serve whether or not He is empowering your work with His Spirit.

Thank God for whatever gifts He has given and commit to using them thoroughly for His glory.

SUNDAY
PRAYER

Father, you have shown me that living the life of Jesus is not a sprint but a marathon. Give me Your pacing for my life. How do I prioritize and how do I accomplish those things that are on Your agenda? Show me how to humbly receive Your gifts, Holy Spirit, and when and how to use them. I need to have Your grace to hear, to listen with my ears of faith and then to say with the boy, Samuel, "Speak, Lord, for your servant is listening." Thank You for hearing me. You are a prayer answering God. I'm grateful. Amen.

WEEK FORTY-EIGHT

Serving Creatively

"True service rests contented in hiddenness. It does not fear the lights and blare of attention, but it does not seek them either . . . the divine nod of approval is completely sufficient."
– Richard Foster

MONDAY

THOUGHTS FOR TODAY

We already have been reflecting on various spiritual gifts and beginning to consider which gift or gifts the Holy Spirit has given to each of us. By now, you may have a pretty good idea of the gifts He has given you. Now how do we know what He wants us to do to use the gifts He has given? There are several steps I recommend:

Pray: We need to spend time in prayer, asking Him to give us a vision for what He wants to do through us as we live our lives in this world. Because we are committed to serving God, we don't want to create a human vision, but, instead, we want to tap into the vision that God has already prepared for us. This will involve asking for His guidance and then waiting patiently in His presence as He begins to show us His plan, usually just one step at a time.

Assess: As we explore and begin to understand God's vision for our service, we may need to assess our passions. What gets us up in the morning, makes our hearts beat a little faster, or brings smiles to our faces? One thing that helps me to assess my passions is to find time in the evening to review, in God's presence, the events of the day, asking questions like these:

- When today did I feel most alive?

- Was there a time when God felt especially close?

- What activity or event brought about the deepest emotional response?

Then, I ask myself these questions:

- What did I observe today that must be faced, embraced, or acted upon?

- What do I feel God is calling me to do more of? Less of?

Over a period of time, we will likely see a pattern emerge revealing the kinds of activities for which God has wired us. Emotions are one part of the way in which God directs our lives. Our feelings matter to us and they matter to Him.

Remember: The next step is to reflect on difficulties we have overcome in our lives. If we have been through divorce, recovery from addiction, financial stresses, health crises, rearing children, or career obstacles, we might be in a good position to help those who are presently facing the same struggles.

People: Finally, as we look around us, do we see someone God has placed in our path who may need the kind of help we can give? Maybe that person is the one on whom we are to begin exercising our spiritual gifts.

TUESDAY

MEDITATION

"For we are God's workmanship, created in Christ Jesus to do good works, which God prepared in advance for us to do." (Ephesians 2:10)

As you meditate on these words, allow the Spirit to give you a vision for the kinds of good works God has prepared for you do to do.

WEDNESDAY

THOUGHTS FOR TODAY

Our attitudes may need to be adjusted if we are going to be able to engage in God's vision for the use of our spiritual gifts. For example, if we have a willingness to serve, we also need to have a *willingness to be interrupted.* Sometimes we are on the path to accomplishing something important and a friend calls who needs a listening ear or a ride to the airport. Humanly, we want to finish what we have started, but God's plans and our plans may be different. Need creates opportunity. Is this one of the good deeds that God has prepared for us to do? We need to ask Him and then proceed accordingly, thanking Him for the divine interruption.

We also need to *guard the use of our tongue.* Part of our service will likely include conversation, advising, teaching, confronting, and listening. We must make sure that when we engage our tongues for these kinds of spiritual service we are doing so under the guidance, and even control, of the Holy Spirit. We must constantly be in prayer as we communicate with those we serve asking that our words, our tone, and our body language bring truth and love to the listener and glory to God. As Paul says, "Do not let any unwholesome talk come out of your mouths, but only what is helpful for building others up according to their needs, that it may benefit those who listen" (Ephesians 4:29).

THURSDAY
THOUGHTS FOR TODAY

As the Spirit begins to open our eyes to needs around us and confirms the gifts we have been given, we will be amazed at the opportunities in front of us. I have a friend who has a helping gift. He is the one who shows up early at church on Sunday to shovel the walks. And he makes sure the coffee is on for the committees and groups that meet during the week. He has done these things for so many years that he doesn't even think about them anymore – he simply sees needs and meets them.

I know of another couple who, with the support of their church, have opened a home where young, unmarried, pregnant girls can stay until their babies are born. While there, the girls receive medical care, counseling, spiritual encouragement, and lots of love. Many have found that what seemed to be a side road in their lives became, instead, a turning point, leading them to eternal relationship with God all because this couple is using the gifts of compassion that God has given them.

As we begin to serve, we will discover where our service best fits in God's overall plan. What begins as a small thing might grow to a full-time ministry. Or, it may multiply into more and more "small" things. And we will not know which of those "small" things may be used by the Spirit for God's glory and for the building of up people in His great family.

FRIDAY
READING GOD'S MESSAGE

Ecclesiastes 4:9-12

As you read these verses about human beings working together, can you think of how your spiritual gifts can help another member of God's family . . .

> . . . in his work? (v. 9)
>
> . . . in his trouble? (v. 10)
>
> . . . in his need? (v. 11)
>
> . . . in his protection? (v. 12)

SATURDAY
FOR PERSONAL REFLECTION

Spend some time in prayer, asking God . . .

to help you know and understand the spiritual gift(s) you have been given, and

to give you a vision for how He wants that gift to be used to serve others.

Ponder these things as you look around for opportunities to serve. Who has a need you can fill? Is there a position in your church for which you are particularly suited? Is there a passion in your heart that can be lived out in serving others?

With the guidance of the Spirit, begin to write out a vision for putting your gift(s) to work in God's kingdom. Then start. Even a small step is a beginning.

SUNDAY
PRAYER

Father, I confess that I have trouble believing that Your creativity is eternal and will never come to an end. You do one creative thing in my life, I am amazed, even giddy over it, and yet think that You won't be able to do that again in another situation or event. I'm sorry that I have limited You by my own limited belief. Let me walk in newness of life and step out boldly knowing that You will creatively walk alongside. I await this newness with great expectation and ask in Your creative power, Jesus. Amen.

WEEK FORTY-NINE

Finding Time to Serve

"We are settling for a Christianity that revolves around catering to ourselves when the central message of Christianity is actually about abandoning ourselves." - David Platt

MONDAY

THOUGHTS FOR TODAY

We will never have extra time to serve God. We must find it. We must make room for it. We must (almost) pull it out of the magician's hat! For most of us, our schedules are already full. If that is the case, the only way to do find the time to use our gifts in God's service may be to give up something else. Meaningful service will always cost us something.

There is a great story in the Old Testament that serves as an example to us. A plague had been sent against Israel, but God stopped the destruction at the threshing floor of Araunah and, as a result, the people of Jerusalem survived. King David was grateful to God and wanted to build an altar of worship on the threshing floor where God's mercy was shown. So he went to Araunah and offered to buy the area around the threshing floor. Araunah, knowing he was talking to the king, said, (essentially), "Just take it. In fact, I will give you animals for sacrifice, too. You don't owe me a thing!"

David's response was this, "I will not sacrifice to the Lord my God burnt offerings that cost me nothing." (2 Samuel 24:24b). So he paid for the land and for the oxen for sacrifice and he worshipped God with a true spirit of service and sacrifice. The end of the story is good, too: The threshing floor of Araunah became the very spot where David's son, Solomon, built a magnificent temple to God. After the temple was destroyed many years later, it was rebuilt (twice over the centuries) on the same spot and there are remains of it in Jerusalem today on Araunah's threshing floor, now part of what is known as the Temple Mount.

God honored David's willingness to offer a sacrifice that cost him something. He will do the same for us. If we give up a place in our schedule for God's service, it will cost us something: relaxation, sleep, going out to eat, watching the movie everybody is talking about, overtime at work, a clean house, or our favorite television program. Maybe we need to remind ourselves of David's comment about wanting his sacrifice to cost him something the next time we are asked to teach a class at church or serve on a committee or help out in a soup kitchen. Maybe we need to think about our true priorities as we see needs around us that we could meet if we were willing to make a personal sacrifice of time, energy, or money. God will honor those who are willing to give up something in order to serve Him.

TUESDAY

MEDITATION

"If any of you wants to serve me, then follow me. Then you'll be where I am, ready to serve at a moment's notice. The Father will honor and reward anyone who serves me." (John 12:26 *The Message*)

Read this verse through a few times, then meditate on what it means, from God's perspective, to be ready and willing to serve. Write down any thoughts that may come to you during your time of meditation.

WEDNESDAY

THOUGHTS FOR TODAY

Setting the right priorities is a challenge for every person in our society who holds a job, runs a household, has a spouse, and/or has children. There are always choices to be made as we look at all the demands on our time. How do we know we are making the right choices? We will probably never be 100% certain of our choices this side of heaven, but I know, because the Bible says so, that when we put God first, making priority decisions becomes easier.

I heard a sermon recently in which the pastor stated that there are some very specific things we can do to make sure God is the first priority in our lives. He said we should give God . . .

... the first day of every week,
... the first half-hour of every day,
... the first 10% of all our money, and
... the first consideration in every decision we make.

That doesn't sound so hard, does it? If we do these simple things, we can be fairly confident that we are putting God in first place and we then will find that other decisions follow in the appropriate order of priority. When our day-to-day priorities put God in first place, we can be assured that we are serving God in the best use of our time, resources, spiritual gifts, and energy.

THURSDAY
THOUGHTS FOR TODAY

There is an interesting concept in the Hebrew culture called *beautifying the commandments*. The idea is that we want to do *more* than God requires so that our service will bring glory to Him. This attitude makes serving him beautiful rather than burdensome. So, now that we have identified the spiritual gifts we have been given and are working on getting our priorities in order, let's think about how we can bring beauty to our service in order to show love to God and to our neighbors.

As we look for ways to serve, remember that one of the best ways to help others is by doing for them something that we already like to do. We tend to find time for things we enjoy doing!

- If we bake cakes, we can bake them as acts of love for people who need a reason to celebrate.
- If we like to fix broken things, we can offer our fix-it abilities to single moms who are forever in need of such services.
- If we are landscapers, we can offer our help to Habitat for Humanity.
- If we are writers, we can write letters or encouraging thoughts to those who are going through times of difficulty.

These are just a few ideas. As we think about our unique gifts and the passions that drive us, we certainly can find creative ways to reach out with enthusiasm and joy to others around us. In that way, we will be beautifying the commands of God and bringing His love to those we serve.

FRIDAY
READING GOD'S MESSAGE

2 Timothy 2:15-22

List the commands that Paul gives to Timothy in these verses:

What do verses 20 and 21 tell us about what we need to do to be useful to God?

With whom should we associate? (v. 22)

What does this passage tell you about how you might be better prepared to serve God?

SATURDAY
FOR PERSONAL REFLECTION

As you look at your weekly schedule, what might you eliminate in order to have some flexible time for serving God?

Where do you see doors of opportunity opening up where you might be able to put your spiritual gift(s) to work? Brainstorm for a few minutes and make a written list.

Then take your ideas in prayer to Him and watch as, through the days and weeks to come, opportunities to be Jesus to others begin to open up. Make sure that all glory for your service goes back to God who created you to serve and to love.

SUNDAY
PRAYER

Jesus, you are a beautiful Savior, you are the King of Creation, Son of God and Son of Man. As I relax in Your presence, I can see You guiding me in the way that I should go. But first, You invite me to rest here with You awhile. You are never in a hurry. Yes, there is urgency, but You never want me to go in haste. You assure me that I will get more done if I rest here with You first. Father, thank you again for sending Your son, Jesus, to take on human flesh so He could relate to us from our vantage point as human beings. I ask for the energy of the Holy Spirit as I go forward holding Your hand. In Your power alone, I ask this. Amen.

WEEK FIFTY

Leading or Following

"As you care less about what people think of you, you will care more about what others think of themselves." – Stephen R. Covey

MONDAY

THOUGHTS FOR TODAY

What do you think of when you think of a leader? We often think of presidents or CEO's or ministers. We tend to think of these people as being exceptionally smart, quite authoritative, and sometimes even dictatorial. They seem to always know the right thing to do and they order people to get it done. That model worked pretty well for Henry the Eighth and it may work in some corporate venues today, but it is not the model that is taught in Scripture. Jesus told His disciples that the one who leads is the one who serves.

We have been talking a lot these weeks about serving. True serving means having an attitude that desires to help others, longs to see people know God as we do, has compassion for those in physical distress, and wants to bring pleasure to God. When we serve this way, Jesus says we are leaders in his kingdom. Over and over again we find that Jesus turns the systems of the world upside down. Leadership is no exception.

Why does Jesus' definition of leadership work so well? I believe it has to do with authority. Serving others gives us the right to be heard. Our willingness to serve opens the hearts of others to listen to what we have to say. God's style of leadership has very little to do with power and has everything to do with authority. Those with quiet authority can move people to accomplish things they never thought possible. Those of us who do not see ourselves as CEO's can be leaders in God's upside-down kingdom by using the gifts and abilities we have to serve others while speaking and acting with the quiet authority based on the Word of God and on the confidence instilled by the Spirit. That is the kind of leadership that has power to change the world.

Aspiring to leadership in God's kingdom is a good thing. It does not mean that we are power-hungry or controlling or autocratic.

Instead, it means downward mobility, moving from positions of power to positions of service. It means valuing a little child as much as we value a political leader. It means looking into the *hearts* of individuals, as Jesus did, instead of judging by outward appearance. Godly leadership means understanding that a small act accomplished in love might have great impact for eternity.

TUESDAY
MEDITATION

". . . whoever wants to become great among you must be your servant, and whoever wants to be first must be slave of all. For even the Son of Man did not come to be served, but to serve, and to give his life as a ransom for many." (Mark 10:43b-45)

Meditate on these verses and allow the Spirit to show you how this message applies to your heart. Write down insights you may be given. Carry the message of this passage with you internally all day today.

WEDNESDAY
THOUGHTS FOR TODAY

Have you ever been asked to take on a leadership position for which you felt unqualified? Most of us are poor judges of our own capabilities. Our initial reaction often is turn down the opportunity to serve. There is only one way to determine if we are to take on a new area of service or not. We must turn to the One who has called us to serve. After all, the Holy Spirit has given us specific, spiritually-empowered gifts to use in His kingdom. He alone knows the best way to put those gifts to work.

Serving without surrounding that service in prayer is like mowing the lawn without turning on the lawn mower. We can expend lots of energy, move around a lot, and even stir up some dust, but we will not be getting the job done. The only jobs that count are those that God has given specifically for us to do. Venturing out without Him is wasted effort.

So, the next time we are asked to take on a new responsibility maybe we should not give an immediate answer. We must ask for time and then take the opportunity to God in prayer. As we wait on Him and the answer will come. We will know whether to say "yes" or "no" to the request and, if we do move forward, it will be under the empowerment and guidance of the Spirit and the work of our hands will be blessed.

THURSDAY
THOUGHTS FOR TODAY

Everybody leads somebody. When we consider our new understanding of leadership as *influence* or *authority* instead of the giving of orders that must be obeyed, we realize that each of us has influence over someone. It may be our children, our neighbors, our best friends, co-workers, or the guy who just fixed our car. The degree of influence we have is directly proportional to the amount of effort we have put into the relationship. If we have earned a person's trust by consistently serving them in love, we have influence and that, according to God, means we are in a position to exercise leadership.

Where are we leading those who follow us? Are we leading them into a relationship with God and into developing their own gifts for service? That kind of leadership requires that we have a vision for what God can do in and through them and then, based upon the confidence given by the Holy Spirit's direction, we share that vision with them. Then we encourage, we build up, we keep serving and, in doing these things, we help to launch those who follow us into their own positions of leadership.

Isn't God's plan great? As Christians we look to each other for leadership, for encouragement, and for confirmation of the vision for our lives. There is no need for hierarchy. God just asks that we be faithful in service. He provides the authority, the confidence, and the influence. He makes us leaders without our even noticing!

FRIDAY
READING GOD'S MESSAGE

John 13:1-17

What was Jesus showing his disciples when He washed their feet? (v.1)

What else was He trying to teach them? (v. 15)

What promise does Jesus give to those who serve? (v. 17)

What would your reaction have been if Jesus had offered to wash your feet?

What does this passage teach us about serving and being served?

SATURDAY
FOR PERSONAL REFLECTION

Is there someone in your life you should be more willing to serve? Who?

What is the barrier that keeps you from willingly serving that person?

Spend some time in prayer asking God to show you the attitude Jesus would have if He were in your place. Then allow the Spirit to infuse you with that mindset. Thank Him for changing you from the inside out.

Then begin to look for opportunities to serve the person about whom you prayed

SUNDAY
PRAYER

Father, thank you for making the ground level at the cross of Jesus, and for saying that the greatest in the Kingdom of God is a servant. Help me to work for Your priorities. Whatever is popular in the world doesn't seem to be popular with You; let me choose what pleases You. This will give me a peaceful demeanor, a confidence in my calling and a contentment with my place in Your Kingdom. I ask for the Comforter to make the truth of Your leadership example real to me. I await Your help, Holy Spirit. Amen

WEEK FIFTY-ONE

Rewards of Serving

"Christians should do what God says is right because in doing it we enjoy more of God." - John Piper

MONDAY
THOUGHTS FOR TODAY

God is the best possible example of an employer. First, He has given us specific abilities and resources that He wants us to put to work in His kingdom. Then, as we reach out to someone in need or try out the talents He has given us, He watches. He encourages, corrects, makes our work effective, and rewards us for trusting Him enough to make His work a priority.

Most of the time, the work we do for our heavenly employer does not result in a weekly paycheck. It's volunteer work. We don't get paid. We do these things because God has asked us to serve Him and those around us. He has given us gifts and talents to be put to work without regard to the monetary cost to us. He is keeping the records and has promised to reward us according to His pay scale.

I knew a couple years ago now who felt that God was directing them to go to Russia as missionaries. Bob and Rene' were truly committed to serving God, but were doing so much for Him here in western Michigan, many of us doubted if they were correctly hearing God's voice. They were sure, though. Bob quit his job as the general manager of a manufacturing company. They sold their beautiful home and most of their possessions. They said their goodbyes to their children and set off across the sea to a not-very-pretty city in Russia. They lived in a walk-up apartment, began to learn the strange language, and developed a love for the Russian people. Over the first few years, Bob and Rene' helped to establish a church and, along with Russian co-workers, taught people who had lived for many years under atheistic Communism about a God who loved them. God rewarded their sacrificial commitment with responsiveness to their message, transformed lives, new friendships, and supernatural joy.

Then the unthinkable happened. Bob was having dinner in a

Russian restaurant one evening when he suffered a massive heart attack and died a short time later. In one instant he was face-to-face with Jesus, the one he had chosen to serve above all others. Do you think at that moment that he was sorry he had given away earthly possessions in order to serve his Creator? No. At that moment Bob saw through Jesus' eyes the eternal value of the choices he had made. I doubt he had any regrets about trading in a nice house in Michigan for unimaginable rewards in heaven!

TUESDAY
MEDITATION

"Serve wholeheartedly, as if you were serving the Lord, not men, because you know that the Lord will reward everyone for whatever good he does . . ." (Ephesians 6:7-8a)

Think about what it means to serve our Lord with total commitment. Allow the Spirit to work this message into your heart. Make a note of any insights you receive.

WEDNESDAY
THOUGHTS FOR TODAY

Sometimes we question whether working for eternal reward is an appropriate motivation. It seems that we should work just to honor God and to accomplish His mission in this world. That should be enough, right? But it is Jesus Himself who has promised to reward us. He says, "Behold I am coming soon! My reward is with me and I will give to everyone according to what he has done" (Revelation 22:12). God is not stingy. He pays extremely well. The Bible is full of promises of reward for using our money, talents, and time in ways that please Him.

Think of your family around the tree on Christmas morning. You have found the perfect gift for your spouse. You simply cannot wait for the package to be opened so you can see the expression on his/her face. I think that is exactly how Jesus feels about the rewards He has promised. He has the perfect gifts picked out for us. He is eagerly waiting for the day when we see Him in eternity and He can watch the expression on our faces as we receive what He has chosen just for us. There will be no need to exchange anything for a different size or color!

Thinking about the rewards we will receive helps to keep us focused on eternity, on pleasing our true Master, and on making value decisions today that help us to invest our earthly treasures into what really matters: loving people by loving and serving God.

THURSDAY
THOUGHTS FOR TODAY

It takes a lot of faith to work for a future reward. We are geared for immediate gratification, fair pay for a job well done, and instant feedback on the work we perform. God has promised eternal compensation (with bonuses!) for the work we do for Him, but I would not be telling the whole story if I didn't tell you that there are also a lot of immediate rewards for serving God.

First, we are rewarded by those we serve. We often receive smiles and appreciation when we are able to meet specific needs. We see changed lives as our helping hand enables others to develop their abilities and take responsibility for their own lives and families. And we see the joy of individuals who have turned their lives over to God and begin an eternal relationship with Him.

Second, we are rewarded by those with whom we serve. The very best of all relationships are those we build with the men and women with whom we share dreams and common goals. The sweetness of shared successes and the support of shared burdens make our lives easier, brighter, and more meaningful. There is nothing like serving Jesus together to cement friendships and create eternal relationships.

Third, there is a closeness to God that we can experience only in the middle of serving Him. Jesus told his disciples that He no longer called them servants, but, instead, called them friends. That reward is one that begins now and never ends.

FRIDAY
READING GOD'S MESSAGE

Proverbs 19:17; 25:21-22; Jeremiah 17:20; Matthew 10:42; 16:24-27; 19:21

Look up each of these verses and, after each one, write down the kind of behavior or activity God promises to reward:

Proverbs 19:17

Proverbs 25:21-22

Jeremiah 17:20

Matthew 10:42

Matthew 16:24-27

Matthew 19:21

Do any of these verses speak particularly to you about changes you need to make in priorities?

SATURDAY
FOR PERSONAL REFLECTION

What earthly rewards are you presently working for?

Are there any earthly values that you might want to trade in for eternal rewards?

What kinds of rewards does God give you on a daily basis in return for your commitment to Him?

Spend some time in prayer, asking God to give you an eternal view of the values you live out. Be open to the Spirit's asking you to give up something for Him. Then happily do it, knowing that your true payday is still ahead.

SUNDAY

PRAYER

Father, let me be a person who is known for working for Jesus. Let this be enough reward for me---to be a follower of Jesus. You have shown me the beauty of a tree, the grace of a swimming swan, the joy of laughter and the experience of Your wellness. Thank you, Holy Spirit, for helping me believe the verse that tells me to seek first Your kingdom and Your righteousness and then all these things will be added to me. You truly are the Spirit of Truth and my constant companion and guide. I am filled with love. Receive my prayer in Love's name. Amen.

WEEK FIFTY-TWO

On Becoming

"Faith is not the clinging to a shrine, but an endless pilgrimage of the heart." – Abraham Joshua Heschel

MONDAY

THOUGHTS FOR TODAY

We live in a constantly changing world. We have new presidents and new political promises. New songs and new movies are released almost daily. There are new products, new medicines, and new diets, all designed to fill our lives with happiness, beauty, and pleasure. There is a reason that the new and the better intrigue us: We want to change. We want to be better than we are right now. We want the new and improved version of who we are. We sense, somewhere deep within, that we can be better, if only we can find tricks or the tools to make us so.

The same is true in the spiritual realm. The goal of our spiritual journey is transformation. We want our daily lives transformed into meaningful days and hours. We want our inner selves to become more and more like Jesus Himself. We want to see the efforts we make in this world infused by the power of God working through us. But there is no trick or product or new method that will help us become what God wants us to be. There is only one way to do it and it is the way that Jesus revealed when He walked on earth. We are to follow Him. Let's see what Jesus taught His disciples about what it meant to follow Him.

First, He told them that following Him meant they would have to deny themselves (Matthew 16:24). *He would now be their first priority.* They would be asked to sacrifice the way of life they had known to this point and to put all their money on Jesus.

Second, He told them that His sheep would follow Him because they would know His voice (John 10:14). As we spend time with Jesus in prayer, meditation, and Bible reading, we will begin to know God well enough to recognize His voice when He is talking to us.

Third, Jesus told His disciples that those who follow Him

would not walk in darkness, but would have the light of life (John 8:12). Because they were close to Him, He would give them insight and understanding that others did not have. They would walk in a wisdom that is not of this world, but is supernaturally given to those who are following closely in His steps.

Last, He promised that those who follow Him would *have something significant to do* (Mark 1:17). We are promised meaningful, transformed lives if we choose to follow Jesus as His disciples did.

TUESDAY
MEDITATION

"I will give you a new heart and put a new spirit in you; I will remove from you your heart of stone and give you a heart of flesh. And I will put my Spirit in you and move you to follow my decrees and be careful go keep my laws." (Ezekiel 36:26-27)

Meditate on these verses and ponder the ways that God has promised to transform us. Make some notes to help you remember what you are learning. Thank Him for working a miracle of grace in your heart.

WEDNESDAY
THOUGHTS FOR TODAY

We have seen that becoming the person God has designed us to be involves, *first, making the decision to follow Jesus* and to make our relationship to Him the all-encompassing priority in our lives. Following God means living in His Word, making it part of our thought, and reading it both for patterns of life that God lays out and for specific direction that He may want to give.

Then, an important way to put into practice following Jesus is to *develop habits of holy living*. There are many passages in the New Testament epistles that spell out very clearly how we Christians should treat each other and that we should live separated and holy lives in this world. We need to get to know those Scriptures and to follow their direction in our day-to-day living.

Finally, we know that we cannot change ourselves, but *we can put ourselves in God's presence so that He can change us.* The practices that we often call spiritual disciplines are means by which we follow closely after Jesus. Just to remind you, some of those practices include prayer, fasting, solitude, simplicity, confession, celebration, meditation, and worship. As we seek God in these ways, He begins to grow us and change us into the image of his own Son, Jesus. We are transformed, not by our own efforts, but by the power of God working within us. Our part simply is to put Him first and to make ourselves available to His life-changing power

THURSDAY
THOUGHTS FOR TODAY

Following Jesus and allowing the power of God to work within us means that we will change. One of the most significant changes we will find as our relationship with God grows in depth is that we will develop a confident faith. We find ourselves speaking out on issues, advising friends, and making decisions with more certainty because we are immersed in Scripture, awash in prayer, and listening for the voice of God as we move through our lives.

God-confidence results and it begins to show in our lives. The sense that we are living on a plane that God desires and we are being guided by His loving eye is rewarding, but even greater is the overwhelming sense that God has us surrounded by His love and will never let us go. A. W. Tozer puts it this way:

> *God is a person, and in the deep of His mighty nature He thinks, wills, enjoys, feels, loves, desires, and suffers as any other person may. . . He communicates with us through the avenues of our minds, our wills, and our emotions. The continuous and unembarrassed interchanges of love and thought between God and the soul of the redeemed man is the throbbing heart of New Testament religion . . . The man who has God for his treasure, has all things in One* (21).

We began our study in Week One realizing that *we are God's precious pearls.* Now we conclude realize that *God is our eternal treasure.* He is everything. There is nothing else that matters.

FRIDAY

READING GOD'S MESSAGE

Psalm 1:2; Colossians 2:2; Philippians 1:9-11; Psalm 138:3; Jeremiah 31:3

Read each of these passages and write next to the verse what it tells you about your relationship with God:

Psalm 1:2

Colossians 2:2

Philippians 1:9-11

Psalm 138:3

Jeremiah 31:3

SATURDAY

FOR PERSONAL REFLECTION

Is it the desire of your heart to please God? Is there any other desire in your heart that is stronger than the desire to please God?

Do people see Jesus in you or do they just see you in you?

How have you understood dying to self in your Christian life? Are you willing to lay down your old self in order for God to restore your true self in Him?

Spend some time in prayer, asking God to reveal any next steps you need to take in being a whole-hearted follower of Jesus.

SUNDAY

PRAYER

Holy Spirit, thank You for making Jesus real to me. I'll never be done mining the depths of this beautiful Savior, King of Kings and Lord of Lords. I'll always have a purpose----to know Jesus better and to be with those who also want to know Him better. I will find them wherever I go in your world, Lord, because you are universal and Your church is everywhere where two or three gather in your name. Thank You for the gift of the Holy Spirit. If You hadn't gone away, Jesus, we would not have the Comforter. What a wonderful plan. The angels of heaven are celebrating with me over such a delightful way to live. Thank you Father, Son and Holy Spirit, the one true God, for revealing Yourself to me. I love You. Amen.

(21) A. W. Tozer, *The Pursuit of God* (Camp Hill, Pennsylvania: Christian Publications, 1982/1993), pp. 13 and 19

BIBLIOGRAPHY

Barna, George. *The Second Coming of the Church.* Nashville, Tennessee: Thomas Nelson, Inc., 1998.

Bolen, Jean Shinoda. *Close to the Bone.* New York, New York: Simon & Schuster, Inc., 1996.

Bridges, Jerry. *The Practice of Godliness.* Colorado Springs, Colorado: NavPress Publishing Group, 1983.

Foster, Richard. *The Celebration of Discipline.* New York, New York: HarperCollins Publishers, 1998.

Griffin, Emilie. *Clinging.* New York, New York: Multi-Media Communications, Inc., 1983.

Lewis, C. S. *A Grief Observed.* New York, New York: The Seabury Press, Inc., 1963.

Lewis, C.S. *Prince Caspian.* New York, New York: HarperCollins, Publishers, Inc., 1979.

Manning, Brennan. *The Ragamuffin Gospel.* Sisters, Oregon: Multnomah Press, 1990.

Moore, Thomas. *Care of the Soul.* New York, New York: HarperCollins Publishers, Inc, 1992.

Peck, M. Scott. *The Road Less Traveled.* New York, New York: Simon & Schuster, Inc., 1978.

Smedes, Lewis B. *Forgive and Forget.* New York, New York: Simon & Schuster, Inc., 1984

Sweet, Leonard. *Soul Salsa.* Grand Rapids, Michigan: Zondervan Publishing House, 2000.

Thomas, Gary. *The Glorious Pursuit.* Colorado Springs, Colorado: NavPress, 1998.

Thomas, Gary. *Sacred Marriage.* Grand Rapids, Michigan: Zondervan Publishing House, 2000.

Tolstoy, Leo. *Walk in the Light and Twenty-Three Tales.* Farmington, Pennsylvania: The Plough Publishing House, 1998.

Tozer, A. W. *The Pursuit of God.* Camp Hill, Pennsylvania: Christian Publications, Inc., 1982

Tverberg, Lois. *Listening to the Language of the Bible.* Holland, Michigan: En-Gedi Resource Center, Inc., 2004.

Vernick, Leslie. *How to Live Right When Your Life Goes Wrong.* Colorado Springs, Colorado: Waterbrook Press, 2003.

Wiederkehr, Macrina. *Seven Sacred Pauses: Living Mindfully Through the Hours of the Day.* Notre Dame, Indiana: Soren Books, 2008.

ABOUT THE AUTHORS

Beverly J. Van Kampen

I am an ordinary person doing life just as you are doing it – one day at a time. Born and raised in western Michigan, I attended Taylor University for two years, studying English, graduating two years after that from Central Michigan University with a degree in education and journalism. Then I completed some graduate studies at Western Michigan University.

Career-wise, I began teaching high school English, then spent two years teaching young adolescents at a school for missionary kids in Honduras. When I returned to the U.S., I was wooed into the world of business and spent nearly a quarter of a century as part of a team creating and growing a commercial real estate development company from our offices in west Michigan.

It was a great run, but demanding. When I was ready to slow down, I left the business world, thinking of an early retirement. After three years of too much quiet, I began volunteering for Our Daily Bread Ministries in their online theological education program. Then I was recruited to be their Director of Online Education, a position I filled for three years, passing the reins to a much more qualified leader in 2014.

I have two grown daughters, and two stepsons, who, together with their amazing spouses, have provided my husband, Warren, and me with eight grandchildren, each of whom, if our predictions are correct, will make significant contributions to solving the world's problems. Yes, they are that smart!

Author with her husband, Warren   Author Marge Lembke

Margery A. Lembke

Margery Lembke, who created the prayers that appear in this devotional, was involved in prayer ministry within the body of Christ for more than 30 years. She served as Prayer Coordinator at Lakeshore Lutheran Fellowship in Spring Lake, Michigan. She also served as a co-leader for Bible studies and spiritual retreats, and engaged in much one-on-one spiritual mentoring throughout her adult life. Margery went to be with the Lord in May of 2015 and her presence and wise counsel are missed by many.

Made in the USA
San Bernardino, CA
09 February 2018